Betty Crocker

BEST

Bisquick® RECIPES

WILEY

Wiley Publishing, Inc.

Library of Congress Cataloging-in-Publication Data:

Crocker, Betty.

Betty Crocker best Bisquick recipes / Betty Crocker.

p. cm.

Includes index.

ISBN 978-0-470-39883-8 (paper : alk. paper)

1. Cookery, American. 2. Quick and easy cookery. 3. Food mixes. I. Title.

TX715.C9213825 2008

641.5'55—dc22

2008022811

Manufactured in the United States of America

10 9 8 7 6 5 4 3 2 1

Cover photo: Classic Strawberry Shortcakes (page 192)

GENERAL MILLS

Publisher, Cookbooks: *Maggie Gilbert/Lynn Vettel*

Manager, Cookbooks: *Lois Tlusty*

Recipe Development and Testing: *Betty Crocker Kitchens*

Photography: *General Mills Photography Studios and Image Library*

WILEY PUBLISHING, INC.

Publisher: *Natalie Chapman*

Executive Editor: *Anne Ficklen*

Production Director: *Diana Cisek*

Cover Design: *Paul Dinovo*

Art Director: *Tai Blanche*

Interior Design: *Holly Wittenberg*

Interior Layout: *Indianapolis Composition Services*

Manufacturing Manager: *Kevin Watt*

The Betty Crocker Kitchens seal guarantees success in your kitchen. Every recipe has been tested on America's Most Trusted Kitchens™ to meet our high standards of reliability, easy preparation and great taste.

Find more great ideas at *BettyCrocker*.com

Dear Friends,

What a great idea!

It all started back in the 1930s as a fast and easy way to make biscuits and now, more than 75 years later, it's a cooking staple. Bisquick baking mix has always been about versatility and ease. Whether you need a quick dinner idea, want to enjoy Saturday morning pancakes with the family, or want to impress your guests with a fun new recipe, Bisquick makes it easy and delicious any day of the week.

This indispensable cookbook brings together tried-and-true classics such as Easy Chicken Pot Pie and Quick Cherry Cobbler, plus new favorites such as Pear and Blue Cheese Tart or Thai Chicken with Spicy Peanut Sauce. And don't forget dessert: whip up an Impossibly Easy Mocha Fudge Cheesecake or everyone's favorite—Classic Strawberry Shortcakes. When time is tight, check out the 30-Minute Meals to get a family-pleasing meal on the table—fast. For evenings when you have more time, gather the family around the table and serve a comforting casserole, pizza or warming pie.

When you have a box of Bisquick on your shelf, you're always ready to answer the question, "What's for dinner?" and make every day special.

Warmly,

Betty Crocker

Contents

Bisquick Q&A

Bisquick is great to have on hand and a snap to use. But some questions still occasionally crop up. Here are some of the most frequently asked questions about Bisquick.

Q: What's the best way to measure Bisquick mix?

A: For best results, spoon Bisquick mix—without sifting—into a dry-ingredient measuring cup, and level with a straight-edged knife or spatula. Don't pack or tap Bisquick mix into the cup.

Q: Can I use Bisquick mix in recipes that call for flour?

A: Because Bisquick mix contains fat and leavening as well as flour, you can't use it as a straight substitute in baked foods, such as cookies and cakes. However, if you want to use Bisquick mix to thicken a stew or gravy, use the same amount of Bisquick mix as you would flour.

Q: How should I store Bisquick mix?

A: To keep Bisquick mix fresh, store it in an airtight container or plastic bag in a cool, dry place, like on your pantry shelf. If you intend to keep it for a long time, store it in the refrigerator or freezer. If frozen, bring it to room temperature before using.

Q: Is Bisquick mix affected by humidity?

A: Bisquick mix reacts to the environment just like any other flour-based product does. In humid conditions, you may find that doughs

and batters are stickier, softer or more fluid. You can add small amounts of Bisquick mix to make the dough or batter easier to work with.

Q: Can I substitute Bisquick Heart Smart® mix for Original Bisquick® mix in my recipes?

A: It depends. Because the formulas are different, the products perform differently in some recipes. The biggest difference is in the amount of water absorbed when preparing doughs and batters. For that reason, we recommend using the type of Bisquick mix called for in the recipe.

Q: *Will Reduced Fat Bisquick recipes work with Bisquick Heart Smart mix?*

A: Yes, all your favorite Reduced Fat Bisquick recipes still work with Bisquick Heart Smart mix.

Q: *Can I double the recipes for Impossibly Easy Pies?*

A: Impossibly Easy Pies, the crustless pies made with Bisquick mix that have been a favorite of Bisquick users since the 1970s, can successfully be doubled. Just double the ingredients for any Impossibly Easy Pie recipe and bake in either two 9-inch pie plates or a 13 × 9 × 2-inch baking dish. If you use the baking dish, bake the pie for about 10 minutes longer than the recipe indicates.

Q: *Can Impossibly Easy Pies be made ahead?*

A: Savory Impossibly Easy Pies may be covered and refrigerated up to 24 hours before baking. You may need to bake longer than the recipe directs—and watch for doneness carefully. Premade pies will have a slightly lower volume because refrigeration decreases the strength of the leavening. We don't recommend preparing sweet Impossibly Easy Pies ahead.

Q: *What's the best way to store Impossibly Easy Pies?*

A: Cool (if warm), cover and immediately refrigerate any remaining cooked pie. It will keep in the refrigerator for up to 3 days.

Q: *Can I reheat leftover Impossibly Easy Pies?*

A: Reheat leftovers in the microwave. Place one slice on a microwavable plate, and cover with waxed paper. Microwave on Medium (50%) for 2 or 3 minutes or until hot.

High-Altitude Baking with Bisquick

The decrease in air pressure at higher altitudes changes the way foods cook and bake. High altitude considerations that affect Bisquick mix include:

- *gases expanding more from the leavening*
- *a decrease in the boiling point of liquids*
- *a faster rate of evaporation*

In baked goods, these changes translate into longer bake times, collapse of product structure and possible overbrowning. Common high altitude adjustments from the sea-level recipe include one or more of the following:

- *increasing oven temperature*
- *longer bake time*
- *adding more Bisquick mix*

In addition, some recipes may require adding flour or decreasing sugar or oil.

There are no hard and fast rules to follow when baking with Bisquick mix at high altitude. Changes to recipes depend upon the food you are baking and the proportion of ingredients. We suggest you use recipes that have been tested and adjusted for high altitude. All of the recipes in this book have been tested at high altitude.

Bisquick Basics Pancakes

Fluffy pancakes are a perfect way to start a morning. Here are some pancake pointers to get you on your way.

1. **Heat** your skillet over medium-high heat, or turn on your griddle to 375°F about 5 minutes before using. Grease the surface with a light coating of vegetable oil. If greasing with cooking spray, spray it before heating. To test the temperature, sprinkle it with a few drops of water. If the water bubbles skittle around before they disappear, the heat is just right.

2. **Stir** the batter with a wire whisk or a fork, just until the ingredients are moistened. Any small lumps in the batter will disappear during cooking.

3. **Test** one pancake so you can see how your pancake batter will act. If the batter is too thin, it will spread unevenly and result in flat pancakes; a too-thick pancake batter won't spread much at all. Add a little milk until the batter reaches the desired consistency.

4. **Repeated** cooking on both sides will toughen the pancakes. Flip the pancakes when they're puffed, covered with bubbles and dry around the edges. Cook the other side until golden brown (the second side never browns as evenly as the first).

5. **Keep** pancakes warm by placing them in a single layer on a wire rack or paper towel-lined cookie sheet in a 200°F oven. Don't stack warm pancakes, or they'll become limp and soggy.

Q: *Why are my pancakes raw in the center?*
A: Too little liquid or too much Bisquick mix may be reasons. Or, your griddle temperature may be too high. For best results, cook pancakes approximately 1 minute 15 seconds on the first side and 1 minute on the second side.

Q: *Can Bisquick mix pancake batter be prepared ahead of time?*
A: Yes, but not too far ahead. Make the batter, then cover and refrigerate no longer than 1 hour.

Q: *Why are my pancakes tough and leathery?*
A: If the temperature is too low, pancakes will take longer to brown and become dry and tough. If the griddle is too hot, the pancakes' edges will be overcooked and tough.

Q: *Can I use buttermilk in pancakes?*
A: Yes, just use the same amount of buttermilk as you would use milk or water for pancakes.

Q: *What's the best way to store leftover pancakes?*
A: Store them in an airtight container or plastic food-storage bag in the refrigerator no longer than 2 days, or freeze for up to 3 months. Microwave individual frozen pancakes on High for 20 to 30 seconds.

Bisquick Basics Waffles

Wow them with wonderful waffles! It's easy—here's how.

1. **Prevent** waffles from sticking by seasoning the waffle iron according to the manufacturer's directions. If greasing with cooking spray, remember to spray it before heating the iron. Starting with a clean waffle iron is also important. After each time you use it, remove all traces of baked-on batter or crumbs.

2. **Mix** the waffle batter right in a 4- or 8-cup glass measuring cup that has a handle and a spout, which makes it easy pouring onto the waffle iron.

3. **The amount** of batter you use depends on the model of your waffle iron. Usually it's a little else than a cupful, but every waffle iron is slightly different. Pour the batter onto the waffle iron so each section of the waffle grid gets covered and it is full but not overflowing. Close the lid and wait. When the iron stops giving off steam, the waffle should be done. Try lifting the lid—if it resists at all, the waffle needs more time to cook.

4. **Lift** the waffle from the iron using a fork. To keep waffles warm until serving time, place them in a single layer on a wire rack or paper towel-lined cookie sheet in a 350°F oven for up to 20 minutes. Don't stack warm waffles, or they'll become soggy.

Bisquick Basics Muffins

Making muffins that look and taste great doesn't involve any magic—just a few quick tips and techniques.

1. **Stir** the batter just until the ingredients are moistened; the batter will look a little lumpy. If you mix the batter too much, the muffins will be tough and the tops will be pointed instead of nicely rounded. Gently fold berries into the batter at the very end to keep the berries from breaking apart and coloring the batter.

2. **Grease** only the bottoms of the muffin cups for nicely shaped muffins with rounded tops and no overhanging edges, or use paper baking cups for easy cleanup.

3. **Divide** the batter evenly among the muffin cups, filling the cups about two-thirds full. Take the guesswork out of filling muffin cups; use a No. 20 or 24 spring-handled ice cream scoop. After filling the cups, wipe up any batter that spills onto the edge of the pan so it won't stick and burn. If you have empty cups in the muffin pan, fill them half full with water so the muffins bake evenly.

4. **Bake** muffins for the shortest time stated in the recipe, then check for doneness. If the muffin tops aren't golden brown or don't spring back when touched lightly in the center, bake a minute or two longer. If the

pan has a dark nonstick finish, you may need to lower the oven temperature by 25°F. If you're using an insulated pan, you may need to increase the baking time slightly. Also, placing the pan on the center oven rack is important so the bottoms of the muffins don't brown too much.

5. **Remove** muffins from the pan immediately so they don't become soggy. Loosen the muffins with a knife or metal spatula, then gently lift. Muffins baked in paper cups should lift right out. Sometimes a recipe will tell you to leave the muffins in the pan for a few minutes so they don't fall apart when you take them out of the pan.

Q: *Why are my muffins peaked and full of holes?*
A: You may have overmixed the batter or your oven temperature may be too high.

Q: *Why didn't my muffins rise?*
A: Your oven temperature may be too low or you may have undermixed the batter.

Q: *What cause muffins to be tough, heavy or rubbery?*
A: Too much egg causes this problem or overmixing.

Bisquick Basics Biscuits

It takes just minutes to stir up a batch of homemade biscuits, with these easy biscuit basics.

1. **Stir** the ingredients until a soft, slightly sticky dough forms. If the dough is too soft to handle, stir in 2 to 4 tablespoons of Bisquick.

2. **Knead** the dough on a surface sprinkled with Bisquick mix. Roll the dough in Bisquick mix to keep it from sticking to the surface. Dipping your fingers into a little Bisquick will keep the dough from sticking to your hands. Shape the dough into a ball, and knead it gently about ten times.

Q: *Why didn't my biscuits rise?*
A: Too much liquid or too little Bisquick mix could be reasons. Too little or too gentle kneading might also be the cause.

Q: *Why are my biscuits tough and hard?*
A: Overmixing or overkneading, oven temperature too high or too long a bake time, overmeasurement of Bisquick mix or undermeasurement of liquid.

Q: *Why is my biscuit dough so sticky?*
A: With the change to a trans fat–free formula, the dough has become a little softer and stickier. You can try working in a little more mix during the kneading stage.

3. **Roll** the dough about ½ inch thick. Here's a trick for rolling dough to the right thickness: Use two sticks, ½ inch thick and about 14 inches long, as a guide. Place the ball of dough between the sticks, and roll the dough to the thickness of the sticks.

4. **Cut** the dough with a round biscuit cutter dipped in Bisquick, pushing the cutter straight down through the dough. If you twist as you cut, the biscuits may be uneven. Cut the biscuits out of the dough as close together as possible. After cutting as many biscuits as possible, lightly press the scraps of dough together. Roll or pat the remaining dough until it is ½ inch thick, then cut. These biscuits may look slightly uneven.

5. **Place** the biscuits about 1 inch apart on an ungreased cookie sheet. Shiny aluminum cookie sheets of good-quality produce the best biscuits. If the cookie sheet is dark, the bottoms of the biscuits will be darker in color. Reducing the oven temperature to 400°F may help. Place the cookie sheet on the center oven rack so the biscuits will brown evenly on both the top and bottom.

CHAPTER 1

Favorite

Breakfasts and Breads

Scrambled Egg Biscuit Cups

PREP TIME: 30 MINUTES ▪ START TO FINISH: 30 MINUTES
12 BISCUIT CUPS

2 cups Original Bisquick® mix

1/3 cup shredded Cheddar cheese (1 1/2 oz)

3/4 cup milk

8 eggs

1/8 teaspoon pepper

1 tablespoon butter or margarine, softened

1/2 cup Parmesan and mozzarella cheese pasta sauce (from 16-oz jar)

3 tablespoons real bacon bits (from 3-oz package or jar)

1 tablespoon chopped fresh chives

Additional real bacon bits, if desired

1 Heat oven to 425°F. Spray bottoms only of 12 regular-size muffin cups with cooking spray. In medium bowl, mix Bisquick mix, cheese and 1/2 cup of the milk until soft dough forms.

2 Place dough on surface sprinkled with Bisquick mix. Shape into a ball; knead 4 or 5 times. Shape into 10-inch roll. Cut roll into 12 pieces. Press each piece in bottom and up side of each muffin cup, forming edge at rim.

3 Bake 8 to 10 minutes or until golden brown. Remove from oven. With back of spoon, press puffed crust in each cup to make indentation.

4 In large bowl, beat eggs, remaining 1/4 cup milk and the pepper until well blended. In 10-inch nonstick skillet, melt butter over medium heat. Add egg mixture. Cook 3 to 4 minutes, stirring occasionally, until firm but still moist. Fold in pasta sauce and bacon until blended.

5 To remove biscuit cups from pan, run knife around edge of cups. Spoon egg mixture into biscuit cups. Sprinkle tops with chives and bacon.

High Altitude (3500–6500 ft): Bake 10 to 12 minutes.

1 BISCUIT CUP: Calories 180 (Calories from Fat 80); Total Fat 9g (Saturated Fat 3.5g); Cholesterol 150mg; Sodium 420mg; Total Carbohydrate 15g (Dietary Fiber 0g); Protein 8g

Breakfast Pinwheels

PREP TIME: 20 MINUTES ■ **START TO FINISH: 40 MINUTES**
12 PINWHEELS

PINWHEELS

2¼ cups Original Bisquick mix

½ cup milk

1 tablespoon butter or margarine, softened

¼ cup granulated sugar

1 teaspoon ground cinnamon

½ cup finely chopped walnuts

½ cup dried currants

1 tablespoon butter or margarine, melted

GLAZE

¾ cup powdered sugar

¼ teaspoon vanilla

1 tablespoon milk

1 Heat oven to 400°F. Line cookie sheet with parchment paper. In medium bowl, stir Bisquick mix and ½ cup milk until soft dough forms. Place dough on surface generously sprinkled with Bisquick mix; roll in Bisquick mix to coat. Knead 5 times.

2 Press or roll dough into 11 × 8-inch rectangle. Spread dough with 1 tablespoon softened butter. In small bowl, mix granulated sugar, cinnamon, walnuts and currants; sprinkle over top of dough; press in slightly. Starting with an 11-inch side, roll up dough tightly; seal edge. Cut into ¾-inch slices. Place slices on cookie sheet. Brush slices with 1 tablespoon melted butter.

3 Bake 8 to 10 minutes or until golden brown. Remove from cookie sheet; cool 10 minutes. In small bowl, mix all glaze ingredients, adding milk, 1 teaspoon at a time, until glaze is thin enough to drizzle. Drizzle glaze over pinwheels. Serve warm.

High Altitude (3500–6500 ft): Bake 13 to 15 minutes.

1 PINWHEEL: Calories 210 (Calories from Fat 70); Total Fat 8g (Saturated Fat 2.5g); Cholesterol 5mg; Sodium 290mg; Total Carbohydrate 32g (Dietary Fiber 1g); Protein 3g

Banana Split Pancakes

PREP TIME: 15 MINUTES ■ **START TO FINISH: 15 MINUTES**
5 SERVINGS (3 PANCAKES EACH)

2 cups Original Bisquick mix

1¼ cups milk

¼ cup chocolate-flavor syrup

1 egg

2 medium bananas, sliced

2 cups sliced strawberries

Whipped topping, if desired

Chopped peanuts, if desired

Additional chocolate-flavor syrup, if desired

Maraschino cherries, if desired

1 In medium bowl, stir Bisquick mix, milk, ¼ cup chocolate-flavor syrup and the egg with wire whisk or fork until blended (batter may be thin).

2 Brush griddle or skillet with vegetable oil or spray with cooking spray; heat griddle to 375°F or heat skillet over medium heat.

3 For each pancake, pour slightly less than ¼ cup batter onto hot griddle. Cook until edges are dry. Turn; cook other sides until golden brown.

4 Serve with bananas, strawberries, whipped topping, peanuts, chocolate-flavor syrup and maraschino cherries.

High Altitude (3500–6500 ft): No change.

1 SERVING: Calories 350 (Calories from Fat 80); Total Fat 9g (Saturated Fat 3g); Cholesterol 45mg; Sodium 640mg; Total Carbohydrate 60g (Dietary Fiber 4g); Protein 8g

Oatmeal Pancakes with Banana-Walnut Syrup

PREP TIME: 30 MINUTES ■ **START TO FINISH: 30 MINUTES**

6 SERVINGS (3 PANCAKES EACH)

BANANA-WALNUT SYRUP

2 tablespoons butter or margarine

1/4 cup chopped walnuts

2 bananas, sliced

1 cup maple-flavored syrup

PANCAKES

2 cups Original Bisquick mix

1/2 cup quick-cooking or old-fashioned oats

2 tablespoons packed brown sugar

1 1/4 cups milk

2 eggs

1 In 1½-quart saucepan, melt butter over medium heat. Cook walnuts in butter, stirring occasionally, until walnuts and butter just begin to brown. Add bananas; stir to coat with butter. Stir in maple-flavored syrup; reduce heat to low. Cook until warm. Keep warm while making pancakes.

2 In medium bowl, stir all pancake ingredients with wire whisk or fork until blended.

3 Brush griddle or skillet with vegetable oil or spray with cooking spray; heat griddle to 375°F or heat skillet over medium heat.

4 For each pancake, pour slightly less than ¼ cup batter onto hot griddle. Cook until edges are dry. Turn; cook other sides until golden brown. Serve with warm syrup.

High Altitude (3500-6500 ft): No change.

1 SERVING: Calories 520 (Calories from Fat 140); Total Fat 15g (Saturated Fat 6g); Cholesterol 85mg; Sodium 590mg; Total Carbohydrate 87g (Dietary Fiber 3g); Protein 9g

Ham and Apple Pancakes

PREP TIME: 30 MINUTES ● **START TO FINISH: 30 MINUTES**
4 SERVINGS (3 PANCAKES EACH)

1 can (21 oz) apple pie filling

2 cups Original Bisquick mix

1 cup milk

2 eggs

¾ cup diced cooked ham

½ cup shredded Cheddar
 cheese (2 oz)

2 medium green onions, sliced
 (2 tablespoons), if desired

Ground cinnamon, if desired

1 In 1-quart saucepan, heat pie filling over low heat, stirring occasionally, until hot. Keep warm while making pancakes.

2 In large bowl, stir Bisquick mix, milk and eggs with wire whisk or fork until blended. Stir in ham, cheese and onions.

3 Brush griddle or skillet with vegetable oil or spray with cooking spray; heat griddle to 375°F or heat skillet over medium heat.

4 For each pancake, pour slightly less than ¼ cup batter onto hot griddle. Cook until edges are dry. Turn; cook other sides until golden brown. Serve with warm pie filling; sprinkle with cinnamon.

High Altitude (3500-6500 ft): No change.

1 SERVING: Calories 570 (Calories from Fat 170); Total Fat 18g (Saturated Fat 8g); Cholesterol 140mg; Sodium 1260mg; Total Carbohydrate 82g (Dietary Fiber 3g); Protein 19g

Puffy Pancakes

PREP TIME: 10 MINUTES ▪ START TO FINISH: 45 MINUTES
8 SERVINGS

⅔ cup water

¼ cup butter or margarine

1 cup Original Bisquick mix

4 eggs

1 can (21 oz) fruit pie filling (any flavor)

Powdered sugar, if desired

1 Heat oven to 400°F. Generously grease 13 × 9-inch baking dish or pan.

2 In 2-quart saucepan, heat water and butter to boiling. Add Bisquick mix all at once. Stir vigorously over low heat about 1 minute or until mixture forms a ball; remove from heat. Beat in eggs, two at a time, beating with spoon after each addition until smooth and glossy. Spread in pan (do not spread up sides).

3 Bake 30 to 35 minutes or until puffed and edges are golden brown. Spread pie filling over pancake. Sprinkle with powdered sugar. Serve immediately.

High Altitude (over 3500 ft): Not recommended.

1 SERVING: Calories 210 (Calories from Fat 90); Total Fat 10g (Saturated Fat 2g); Cholesterol 105mg; Sodium 320mg; Total Carbohydrate 27g (Dietary Fiber 1g); Protein 4g

Sausage-Cheese Pancake Sandwiches

PREP TIME: 20 MINUTES ▪ **START TO FINISH: 20 MINUTES**

4 SANDWICHES

1 cup Original Bisquick mix

½ cup milk

2 tablespoons maple-flavored syrup

3 eggs

4 cooked pork sausage patties

1 tablespoon milk

1 teaspoon butter or margarine

4 slices (²/₃ oz each) process American cheese

1 In medium bowl, stir Bisquick mix, ½ cup milk, the maple syrup and 1 of the eggs with wire whisk or fork until blended.

2 Brush griddle or skillet with vegetable oil or spray with cooking spray; heat griddle to 375°F or heat skillet over medium heat.

3 For each pancake, pour 2 tablespoons batter onto hot griddle (make 8 pancakes total). Cook until edges are dry. Turn; cook other sides until golden brown.

4 Meanwhile, heat sausage patties as directed on package. In small bowl, beat remaining 2 eggs and 1 tablespoon milk. In 8-inch nonstick skillet, melt butter over medium heat. Cook eggs in butter, stirring occasionally, until set.

5 For each sandwich, place 1 sausage patty on 1 pancake; top with one-fourth of the eggs, 1 slice cheese and another pancake.

High Altitude (3500-6500 ft): No change.

1 SANDWICH: Calories 410 (Calories from Fat 220); Total Fat 25g (Saturated Fat 10g); Cholesterol 200mg; Sodium 930mg; Total Carbohydrate 29g (Dietary Fiber 0g); Protein 16g

Chocolate Waffles
with Caramel-Banana Topping

PREP TIME: 10 MINUTES ▪ START TO FINISH: 15 MINUTES
6 SERVINGS (TWO 4-INCH WAFFLES EACH)

CARAMEL-BANANA TOPPING

½ cup packed brown sugar

¼ cup whipping (heavy) cream

¼ cup light corn syrup

2 tablespoons butter or margarine

1 teaspoon vanilla

3 medium bananas, sliced

WAFFLES

1½ cups Original Bisquick mix

1 cup sugar

⅓ cup baking cocoa

¾ cup water

2 tablespoons vegetable oil

2 eggs

1 In 1-quart saucepan, mix all topping ingredients except bananas. Heat to boiling, stirring occasionally; remove from heat. Add bananas; stir gently until well coated; keep warm.

2 Heat waffle maker. (Waffle makers without a nonstick coating may need to be brushed with vegetable oil or sprayed with cooking spray.) In medium bowl, stir remaining ingredients until blended.

3 For each waffle, pour batter onto center of hot waffle maker. (Check manufacturer's directions for recommended amount of batter.) Close lid of waffle maker. Bake about 5 minutes or until steaming stops. Carefully remove waffle. Serve with topping.

High Altitude (3500–6500 ft): No change.

1 SERVING: Calories 560 (Calories from Fat 160); Total Fat 18g (Saturated Fat 7g); Cholesterol 90mg; Sodium 500mg; Total Carbohydrate 97g (Dietary Fiber 3g); Protein 6g

Dreamy Orange Waffles

PREP TIME: 35 MINUTES ■ START TO FINISH: 35 MINUTES
6 SERVINGS (TWO 4-INCH WAFFLES EACH)

ORANGE SYRUP

1 cup packed brown sugar

2 tablespoons cornstarch

1 cup orange juice

1 can (11 oz) mandarin orange
　segments, drained

WAFFLES

2 cups Original Bisquick mix

1¼ cups milk

2 tablespoons butter or
　margarine, melted

1 tablespoon grated orange peel

1 egg

TOPPING

1 cup frozen (thawed) whipped
　Topping

1 In 1-quart saucepan, heat brown sugar, cornstarch and orange juice to boiling over medium-high heat, stirring frequently. Boil and stir 1 to 2 minutes or until syrup is slightly thickened and mixture is clear. Remove from heat; stir in orange segments. Keep warm while making waffles.

2 Heat waffle maker. (Waffle makers without a nonstick coating may need to be brushed with vegetable oil or sprayed with cooking spray.) In medium bowl, stir all waffle ingredients with wire whisk or fork until blended.

3 For each waffle, pour batter onto center of hot waffle maker. (Check manufacturer's directions for recommended amount of batter.) Close lid of waffle maker. Bake 3 to 5 minutes or until steaming stops. Carefully remove waffle.

4 Spoon syrup over waffles; top with whipped topping.

High Altitude (3500–6500 ft): No change.

1 SERVING: Calories 460 (Calories from Fat 120); Total Fat 13g (Saturated Fat 7g); Cholesterol 50mg; Sodium 570mg; Total Carbohydrate 78g (Dietary Fiber 2g); Protein 7g

Whole Wheat-Granola Waffles

PREP TIME: 55 MINUTES ■ START TO FINISH: 55 MINUTES
6 SERVINGS (TWO 4-INCH WAFFLES EACH)

2 cups Original Bisquick mix

$\frac{1}{2}$ cup whole wheat flour

$\frac{1}{2}$ cup granola

1$\frac{1}{2}$ cups milk

2 tablespoons packed brown sugar

2 tablespoons vegetable oil

1 egg

1$\frac{1}{2}$ cups fresh berries (raspberries, blueberries, sliced strawberries)

$\frac{3}{4}$ cup maple-flavored syrup

1 Heat waffle maker. (Waffle makers without a nonstick coating may need to be brushed with vegetable oil or sprayed with cooking spray.) In medium bowl, stir all ingredients except berries and syrup with wire whisk or fork until blended.

2 For each waffle, pour batter onto center of hot waffle maker. (Check manufacturer's directions for recommended amount of batter.) Close lid of waffle maker. Bake 3 to 5 minutes or until steaming stops. Carefully remove waffle.

3 Serve waffles with berries and syrup.

High Altitude (3500–6500 ft): No change.

1 SERVING: Calories 480 (Calories from Fat 120); Total Fat 13g (Saturated Fat 3.5g); Cholesterol 40mg; Sodium 560mg; Total Carbohydrate 81g (Dietary Fiber 4g); Protein 9g

Cornbread Waffles
with Apple-Cinnamon Syrup

PREP TIME: 30 MINUTES ▪ START TO FINISH: 30 MINUTES
6 SERVINGS (TWO 4-INCH WAFFLES EACH)

APPLE-CINNAMON SYRUP

1 cup cinnamon apple pie filling (from 21-oz can)

1 cup maple-flavored syrup

WAFFLES

1½ cups Original Bisquick mix

½ cup cornmeal

1 teaspoon ground cinnamon

1⅓ cups fat-free (skim) milk

2 tablespoons canola or soybean oil

1 egg or ¼ cup fat-free egg product

1 In medium microwavable bowl, mix pie filling and maple syrup. Microwave uncovered on High 2 to 3 minutes or until warm; set aside.

2 Heat waffle maker. (Waffle makers without a nonstick coating may need to be brushed with vegetable oil or sprayed with cooking spray.) In medium bowl, stir all waffle ingredients with wire whisk or fork until blended.

3 For each waffle, pour batter onto center of hot waffle maker. (Check manufacturer's directions for recommended amount of batter.) Close lid of waffle maker. Bake 3 to 5 minutes or until steaming stops. Carefully remove waffle. Serve waffles with syrup.

High Altitude (3500–6500 ft): No change.

1 SERVING: Calories 440 (Calories from Fat 90); Total Fat 10g (Saturated Fat 2g); Cholesterol 35mg; Sodium 430mg; Total Carbohydrate 83g (Dietary Fiber 2g); Protein 6g

Do-Ahead Breakfast Bake

PREP TIME: 15 MINUTES ■ START TO FINISH: 5 HOURS
12 SERVINGS

1 cup diced cooked ham

2 boxes (5.2 oz each) hash brown potatoes

1 medium green bell pepper, chopped (1 cup)

1 tablespoon dried chopped onion

2 cups shredded Cheddar cheese (8 oz)

1 cup Original Bisquick mix

½ teaspoon pepper

3 cups milk

4 eggs

1 Spray 13 × 9-inch (3-quart) glass baking dish with cooking spray. In baking dish, mix ham, uncooked potatoes, bell pepper, onion and 1 cup of the cheese; spread evenly.

2 In medium bowl, stir Bisquick mix, pepper, milk and eggs with wire whisk or fork until blended. Pour over potato mixture. Sprinkle with remaining cheese. Cover; refrigerate at least 4 hours but no longer than 24 hours.

3 Heat oven to 375°F. Uncover and bake 30 to 35 minutes or until light golden brown around edges and cheese is melted. Let stand 10 minutes before serving.

High Altitude (3500–6500 ft): No change.

1 SERVING: Calories 280 (Calories from Fat 110); Total Fat 12g (Saturated Fat 6g); Cholesterol 100mg; Sodium 870mg; Total Carbohydrate 29g (Dietary Fiber 2g); Protein 14g

Overnight Blintz Bake

PREP TIME: 15 MINUTES ■ **START TO FINISH: 9 HOURS 25 MINUTES**
12 SERVINGS

FILLING

1 container (15 oz) ricotta
cheese

1 container (8 oz) pineapple
cream cheese spread

2 tablespoons sugar

1 teaspoon vanilla

2 eggs

BATTER

1 cup Original Bisquick mix

1 cup sour cream

$\frac{1}{2}$ cup sugar

$\frac{1}{4}$ cup butter or margarine,
softened

$\frac{1}{2}$ cup pineapple juice

6 eggs

TOPPINGS

$\frac{1}{2}$ cup sour cream

$\frac{3}{4}$ cup strawberry preserves

1 Spray 13 × 9-inch (3-quart) glass baking dish with cooking spray. In medium bowl, stir all filling ingredients until well blended; set aside.

2 In medium bowl, stir all batter ingredients with wire whisk or fork until well blended. Pour batter into baking dish. Pour filling evenly over batter. Cover; refrigerate at least 8 hours or overnight.

3 Heat oven to 325°F. Uncover baking dish; bake 55 to 60 minutes or until golden brown and center is set. Let stand 10 minutes before serving. Top servings with sour cream and strawberry preserves.

High Altitude (3500–6500 ft): Increase Bisquick mix to 1¼ cups. Bake 1 hour to 1 hour 5 minutes.

1 SERVING: Calories 390 (Calories from Fat 200); Total Fat 22g (Saturated Fat 13g); Cholesterol 200mg; Sodium 380mg; Total Carbohydrate 36g (Dietary Fiber 0g); Protein 11g

Cheesy Chile and Egg Bake

PREP TIME: 15 MINUTES ▪ **START TO FINISH: 1 HOUR 5 MINUTES**
12 SERVINGS

1 package (12 oz) bulk pork sausage

1 bag (28 oz) frozen potatoes O'Brien with onions and peppers, thawed, drained

1 can (4.5 oz) chopped green chiles, drained

2 cups shredded Monterey Jack cheese with jalapeño peppers (8 oz)

1/2 cup Original Bisquick mix

1 teaspoon salt

1 1/4 cups milk

1 container (8 oz) sour cream

8 eggs, slightly beaten

1 cup tortilla chips, crushed (1/2 cup)

1 Heat oven to 350°F. In 10-inch skillet, cook sausage over medium-high heat 8 to 10 minutes, stirring occasionally, until thoroughly cooked; drain.

2 In ungreased 13 × 9-inch (3-quart) glass baking dish, mix sausage, uncooked potatoes, chiles and 1 cup of the cheese.

3 In large bowl, beat Bisquick mix, salt, milk, sour cream and eggs with wire whisk or fork until blended. Pour over potato mixture.

4 Bake uncovered 35 to 45 minutes or until knife inserted in center comes out clean. Sprinkle with crushed chips and remaining 1 cup cheese. Bake about 5 minutes longer or until cheese is melted.

High Altitude (3500–6500 ft): Bake 45 to 55 minutes.

1 SERVING: Calories 300 (Calories from Fat 160); Total Fat 18g (Saturated Fat 8g); Cholesterol 185mg; Sodium 640mg; Total Carbohydrate 20g (Dietary Fiber 1g); Protein 14g

Savory Apple Brunch Bake

PREP TIME: 10 MINUTES ■ **START TO FINISH: 45 MINUTES**
8 SERVINGS

1 lb bacon

1 medium unpeeled cooking apple (Rome Beauty, Golden Delicious or Greening), peeled and chopped (1 cup)

2 tablespoons sugar

1½ cups Original Bisquick mix

1½ cups milk

4 eggs

2 cups shredded Cheddar cheese (8 oz)

1 Heat oven to 375°F. Grease rectangular 11 × 7-inch baking dish. In 12-inch skillet, cook bacon over medium heat, turning occasionally, until crisp; drain on paper towels and cool. Crumble bacon into small pieces.

2 In baking dish, mix apple and sugar. Stir Bisquick mix, milk and eggs until blended; pour over apple. Sprinkle with bacon and cheese.

3 Bake uncovered 30 to 35 minutes or until knife inserted in center comes out clean.

High Altitude (3500–6500 ft): No change.

1 SERVING: Calories 370 (Calories from Fat 215); Total Fat 24g (Saturated Fat 11g); Cholesterol 150mg; Sodium 800mg; Total Carbohydrate 22g (Dietary Fiber 1g); Protein 18g

Berry-Banana Bread

PREP TIME: 15 MINUTES ▪ **START TO FINISH: 1 HOUR 25 MINUTES**
1 LOAF (16 SLICES)

2 cups Bisquick Heart
  Smart® mix

3/4 cup quick-cooking oats

2/3 cup sugar

1 cup mashed very ripe bananas
  (2 medium)

1/2 cup fat-free cholesterol-free
  egg product, 4 egg whites or
  2 eggs

1/4 cup fat-free (skim) milk

1 cup fresh or frozen (rinsed and
  drained) blueberries

1 Heat oven to 350°F. Grease bottom only of 9 × 5-inch loaf pan.

2 In large bowl, stir Bisquick mix, oats, sugar, bananas, egg product and milk until moistened; beat vigorously 30 seconds. Fold in blueberries. Pour into pan.

3 Bake 55 to 60 minutes or until toothpick inserted in center comes out clean. Cool 10 minutes. Loosen sides of loaf from pan; remove from pan to cooling rack. Cool completely, about 1 hour, before slicing.

High Altitude (over 3500 ft): Not recommended.

1 SLICE: Calories 120 (Calories from Fat 10); Total Fat 1g (Saturated Fat 0g); Cholesterol 0mg; Sodium 180mg; Total Carbohydrate 26g (Dietary Fiber 1g); Protein 3g

Apple Cake

PREP TIME: 15 MINUTES ▪ **START TO FINISH: 50 MINUTES**
9 SERVINGS

2 cups Original Bisquick mix

½ cup sugar

½ cup milk

2 tablespoons butter or
    margarine, softened

1 egg

1 medium unpeeled red apple,
    thinly sliced (about 1 cup)

¼ cup butter or margarine,
    melted

½ teaspoon ground cinnamon

1 Heat oven to 400°F. Spray 9-inch square pan with cooking spray. In medium bowl, stir Bisquick mix, 2 tablespoons sugar, the milk, butter and the egg until well blended. Spread batter evenly in pan.

2 Arrange apple slices in 3 rows, overlapping slices slightly, on batter. Brush ¼ cup melted butter over tops of apple slices.

3 In small bowl, mix remaining 2 tablespoons sugar and the cinnamon; sprinkle over apples.

4 Bake 16 to 18 minutes or until edges are golden brown. Cool 15 minutes before serving. Cut with serrated knife into 9 squares.

High Altitude (3500–6500 ft): Bake 18 to 20 minutes.

1 SERVING: Calories 220 (Calories from Fat 110); Total Fat 12g (Saturated Fat 6g); Cholesterol 45mg; Sodium 390mg; Total Carbohydrate 25g (Dietary Fiber 1g); Protein 3g

Fruit Swirl Coffee Cake

PREP TIME: 10 MINUTES ■ **START TO FINISH: 35 MINUTES**

18 SERVINGS

4 cups Original Bisquick mix

1/2 cup granulated sugar

1/4 cup butter or margarine, melted

1/2 cup milk

2 teaspoons vanilla

3 eggs

1 can (21 oz) fruit pie filling (any flavor)

1 cup powdered sugar

2 tablespoons milk

1 Heat oven to 350°F. Grease 15 × 10 × 1-inch pan or two 9-inch square pans. In large bowl, stir Bisquick mix, granulated sugar, butter, milk, vanilla, and eggs until blended; beat vigorously 30 seconds.

2 Spread two-thirds of the batter (about 2½ cups) in rectangular pan or one-third of the batter (about 1¼ cups) in each square pan. Spread pie filling over batter (filling may not cover batter completely). Drop remaining batter by tablespoonfuls onto pie filling.

3 Bake 20 to 25 minutes or until golden brown. Mix powdered sugar and 2 tablespoons milk until smooth; drizzle over warm coffee cake. Serve warm or cool.

High Altitude (3500–6500 ft): Heat oven to 375°F. Use 9-inch square pans. Use 3½ cups Bisquick mix. Stir 1/4 cup plus 2 tablespoons all-purpose flour into Bisquick mix. Bake about 25 minutes.

1 SERVING: Calories 220 (Calories from Fat 65); Total Fat 7g (Saturated Fat 2g); Cholesterol 35mg; Sodium 430mg; Total Carbohydrate 37g (Dietary Fiber 1g); Protein 3g

Double-Streusel Coffee Cake

PREP TIME: 15 MINUTES ◉ **START TO FINISH: 1 HOUR 15 MINUTES**
6 SERVINGS

STREUSEL

⅔ cup Original Bisquick mix

⅔ cup packed brown sugar

1 teaspoon ground cinnamon

3 tablespoons firm butter or
  margarine

COFFEE CAKE

2 cups Original Bisquick mix

½ cup milk or water

2 tablespoons granulated sugar

1½ teaspoons vanilla egg

1 Heat oven to 375°F. Spray bottom and side of 9-inch round cake pan with cooking spray. In small bowl, mix ⅔ cup Bisquick mix, the brown sugar and cinnamon. Cut in butter, using pastry blender (or pulling 2 table knives through ingredients in opposite directions), until mixture looks like fine crumbs; set aside.

2 In medium bowl, stir all coffee cake ingredients until blended. Spread about 1 cup of the batter in pan. Sprinkle with about ¾ cup of the streusel. Drop remaining batter over top of streusel; spread carefully over streusel. Sprinkle remaining streusel over top.

3 Bake 20 to 24 minutes or until golden brown. Let stand 30 minutes before serving. Serve warm or cool.

High Altitude (3500–6500 ft): No change.

1 SERVING: Calories 410 (Calories from Fat 120); Total Fat 14g (Saturated Fat 6g); Cholesterol 50mg; Sodium 720mg; Total Carbohydrate 64g (Dietary Fiber 1g); Protein 6g

Carrot-Walnut Coffee Cake

PREP TIME: 15 MINUTES ▪ START TO FINISH: 1 HOUR 20 MINUTES
9 SERVINGS

STREUSEL

1/2 cup Original Bisquick mix

1/3 cup packed brown sugar

2 tablespoons firm butter or margarine

COFFEE CAKE

2 cups Original Bisquick mix

2 tablespoons granulated sugar

1 1/2 teaspoons pumpkin pie spice

1/2 cup chopped walnuts

1/2 cup shredded carrots

1/2 cup raisins

2/3 cup milk

2 tablespoons vegetable oil

1 egg

1 Heat oven to 375°F. In small bowl, mix ½ cup Bisquick mix and the brown sugar until well blended. Cut in butter, using pastry blender (or pulling 2 table knives through ingredients in opposite directions), until mixture looks like fine crumbs; set aside.

2 In large bowl, stir 2 cups Bisquick mix, the granulated sugar, pumpkin pie spice, walnuts, carrots and raisins. Stir in milk, oil and egg with wire whisk or fork until blended. Pour into ungreased 8-inch square pan. Sprinkle with streusel.

3 Bake 30 to 35 minutes or until toothpick inserted in center comes out clean. Cool 30 minutes before serving. Serve warm.

High Altitude (3500–6500 ft): Increase eggs to 2. Bake 38 to 43 minutes.

1 SERVING: Calories 320 (Calories from Fat 140); Total Fat 15g (Saturated Fat 4g); Cholesterol 30mg; Sodium 450mg; Total Carbohydrate 41g (Dietary Fiber 2g); Protein 5g

Buttons and Bows

PREP TIME: 15 MINUTES ▪ **START TO FINISH: 25 MINUTES**
8 BUTTONS AND BOWS

2 cups Original Bisquick mix

2 tablespoons sugar

1 teaspoon ground nutmeg

1/8 teaspoon ground cinnamon

1/3 cup milk

1 egg

1/4 cup butter or margarine, melted

1/2 cup sugar

1 Heat oven to 400°F. In medium bowl, stir Bisquick mix, 2 tablespoons of the sugar, the nutmeg, cinnamon, milk and egg until soft dough forms.

2 Place dough on surface sprinkled with Bisquick mix. Roll dough into a ball; knead about 5 times. Press or roll dough until 1/2 inch thick. Cut dough with doughnut cutter dipped in Bisquick mix. To make bow shapes, hold opposite sides of each ring of dough, then twist to make a figure 8. On ungreased cookie sheet, place bows and buttons (the dough from the center of each ring).

3 Bake 8 to 10 minutes or until light golden brown. Immediately dip each bow and button in melted butter, then in 1/2 cup sugar. Serve warm.

High Altitude (3500–6500 ft): No change.

1 BUTTON AND BOW: Calories 250 (Calories from Fat 90); Total Fat 10g (Saturated Fat 5g); Cholesterol 45mg; Sodium 420mg; Total Carbohydrate 36g (Dietary Fiber 0g); Protein 3g

Coconut, Pineapple and Macadamia Scones

PREP TIME: 15 MINUTES ■ **START TO FINISH: 30 MINUTES**

12 SCONES

2¹/₂ cups Original Bisquick mix

¹/₄ cup sugar

¹/₄ cup firm butter or margarine

¹/₂ cup flaked coconut

¹/₂ cup chopped macadamia nuts

¹/₄ cup whipping cream

1 egg

1 can (8 oz) pineapple tidbits, well drained

1 Heat oven to 425°F. Spray cookie sheet with cooking spray. In large bowl, mix Bisquick mix and sugar. Cut in butter, using pastry blender (or pulling 2 table knives through mixture in opposite directions), until mixture looks like fine crumbs. Stir in remaining ingredients.

2 Pat dough into 10 × 7-inch rectangle on cookie sheet (if dough is sticky, dip fingers in Bisquick mix). Cut into 12 rectangles, but do not separate. Sprinkle with additional sugar and coconut if desired.

3 Bake 12 to 14 minutes or until golden brown; carefully separate rectangles. Serve warm.

High Altitude: (3500-6500 ft): Bake 14 to 16 minutes.

1 SCONE: Calories 230 (Calories from Fat 120); Total Fat 14g (Saturated Fat 6g); Cholesterol 35mg; Sodium 400mg; Total Carbohydrate 24g (Dietary Fiber 1g;); Protein 3g

CHAPTER 2

Easy
Appetizers

Broccoli-Cheddar Appetizers

PREP TIME: 15 MINUTES ▪ **START TO FINISH: 1 HOUR 10 MINUTES**

30 APPETIZERS

1 box (10 oz) frozen chopped broccoli, thawed, drained

1 can (7 oz) vacuum-packed whole kernel corn, drained

1 small onion, chopped (about 1/4 cup)

1/2 cup coarsely chopped walnuts

1/2 cup Original Bisquick mix

1/4 teaspoon garlic salt

1/2 cup milk

1/4 cup butter or margarine, melted

2 eggs

1 cup shredded Cheddar cheese (4 oz)

1 Heat oven to 375°F. Spray 9-inch square pan with cooking spray. In pan, mix broccoli, corn, onion and walnuts.

2 In medium bowl, stir all remaining ingredients except cheese with wire whisk or fork until blended. Pour into pan.

3 Bake 23 to 25 minutes or until knife inserted in center comes out clean. Sprinkle with cheese. Bake 2 to 3 minutes longer or until cheese is melted. Cool 30 minutes. To serve, cut into 5 rows by 3 rows; cut each rectangle diagonally in half.

High Altitude (3500–6500 ft): No change.

1 APPETIZER: Calories 70 (Calories from Fat 45); Total Fat 5g (Saturated Fat 2g); Cholesterol 20mg; Sodium 90mg; Total Carbohydrate 4g (Dietary Fiber 0g); Protein 2g

Pear and Blue Cheese Tart

PREP TIME: 20 MINUTES ■ START TO FINISH: 1 HOUR 10 MINUTES
12 SERVINGS

CRUST

1½ cups Original Bisquick mix

⅓ cup very hot water

FILLING

2 tablespoons butter or margarine

2 shallots, finely chopped (about ⅓ cup)

2 medium pears, peeled, cut into ¼-inch slices (about 2 cups)

¼ cup chopped walnuts

½ cup crumbled blue cheese (2 oz)

2 tablespoons chopped fresh parsley

1 Heat oven to 425°F. Spray 9-inch tart pan with removable bottom with cooking spray.

2 In medium bowl, stir Bisquick mix and hot water until soft dough forms. Press dough in bottom and up side of tart pan, using fingers coated with Bisquick mix. Bake 10 minutes.

3 Meanwhile, in 8-inch skillet, melt butter over medium heat. Add shallots; cook 2 to 4 minutes, stirring occasionally, until tender; remove from heat.

4 Arrange pear slices on crust. Spread butter mixture over pears. Bake 20 minutes.

5 Sprinkle walnuts over pears. Bake about 10 minutes longer or until tart is golden brown.

6 Remove from oven; sprinkle with cheese. Cool 10 minutes on cooling rack. Sprinkle with parsley. Serve warm or at room temperature.

High Altitude (3500–6500 ft): No change.

1 SERVING: Calories 130 (Calories from Fat 60); Total Fat 7g (Saturated Fat 3g); Cholesterol 10mg; Sodium 260mg; Total Carbohydrate 15g (Dietary Fiber 1g); Protein 3g

Apple and Blue Cheese Tart: Substitute 2 medium cooking apples for the pears.

Two-Cheese Straws

PREP TIME: 15 MINUTES ■ **START TO FINISH: 35 MINUTES**
36 APPETIZERS

2½ cups Original Bisquick mix

⅔ cup milk

½ cup shredded Cheddar cheese (2 oz)

1 tablespoon butter or margarine, softened

2 tablespoons grated Parmesan cheese

Tomato pasta sauce, if desired, heated

1 Heat oven to 400°F. Spray cookie sheets with cooking spray. In large bowl, stir Bisquick mix, milk and Cheddar cheese until soft dough forms.

2 Divide dough in half. On surface lightly sprinkled with Bisquick mix, roll 1 half into 9 × 6-inch rectangle. Spread with half of the butter. Sprinkle 1 tablespoon of the Parmesan cheese over top. Cut dough lengthwise into 18 (½-inch) strips. Repeat with remaining dough.

3 Twist each dough strip as many times as possible; place on cookie sheets. Bake 6 to 8 minutes or until light golden brown. Serve with pasta sauce.

High Altitude (3500–6500 ft): Heat oven to 425°F. Bake 8 to 10 minutes.

1 APPETIZER: Calories 45 (Calories from Fat 20); Total Fat 2g (Saturated Fat 1g); Cholesterol 0mg; Sodium 120mg; Total Carbohydrate 6g (Dietary Fiber 0g); Protein 1g

Mini Corn Cakes

PREP TIME: 25 MINUTES ■ START TO FINISH: 25 MINUTES
24 APPETIZERS

1 tablespoon butter or margarine

1/3 cup chopped green onions (about 5 medium)

1/3 cup chopped celery

1/3 cup chopped red bell pepper

1 cup soft white bread crumbs (about 1 1/2 slices bread)

1/2 cup Original Bisquick mix

1 teaspoon sugar

1/2 teaspoon salt

1/8 teaspoon ground red pepper (cayenne)

2 eggs, slightly beaten

1 can (11 oz) whole kernel corn, drained

2 tablespoons vegetable oil

1/2 cup chive-and-onion sour cream

1 In 12-inch nonstick skillet, melt butter over medium heat. Add onions, celery and bell pepper; cook 3 minutes, stirring occasionally.

2 In medium bowl, stir vegetable mixture and remaining ingredients except oil and sour cream until well blended.

3 In same skillet, heat 2 teaspoons of the oil over medium heat. Cooking 8 corn cakes at a time, drop corn mixture into oil by tablespoonfuls, spreading each into 1 1/2–inch round. Cook 1 minute to 1 minute 30 seconds on each side, carefully turning once, until golden brown. Cook remaining corn cakes, using 2 teaspoons oil for each batch of 8 corn cakes. Serve with sour cream.

High Altitude (3500–6500 ft): In step 3, use medium-high heat.

1 APPETIZER (WITH 1 TEASPOON SOUR CREAM): Calories 60 (Calories from Fat 30); Total Fat 3.5g (Saturated Fat 1.5g); Cholesterol 20mg; Sodium 135mg; Total Carbohydrate 6g (Dietary Fiber 0g); Protein 1g

Olive and Ham Appetizer Stacks

PREP TIME: 35 MINUTES ▪ **START TO FINISH: 35 MINUTES**
48 APPETIZERS

1 cup Original Bisquick mix

1 teaspoon dried basil leaves

⅓ cup spicy hot vegetable juice

1 package (8 oz) deli ham slices
(8 thin slices)

48 pimiento-stuffed green
olives

1 Heat oven to 400°F. In medium bowl, stir Bisquick mix, basil and vegetable juice until soft dough forms; beat vigorously 20 strokes. Place dough on surface sprinkled with Bisquick mix; roll in Bisquick mix to coat. Shape into a ball; knead 5 times.

2 Press or roll dough about ¼ inch thick. With 1¼-inch round cutter, cut into rounds. Gather dough scraps together and reroll; cut to make 48 rounds. On ungreased cookie sheets, place dough rounds 1-inch apart.

3 Bake 6 to 8 minutes or until edges begin to turn golden brown. Remove from cookie sheet to cooling rack. Cool 10 minutes.

4 Cut each ham slice into 6 wedge-shaped pieces; roll up each wedge. For each appetizer, spear toothpick into olive, 1 piece of rolled-up ham and baked round.

High Altitude (3500–6500 ft): No change.

1 APPETIZER: Calories 25 (Calories from Fat 10); Total Fat 1g (Saturated Fat 0g); Cholesterol 0mg; Sodium 150mg; Total Carbohydrate 2g (Dietary Fiber 0g); Protein 1g

Sausage-Stuffed Mushrooms

PREP TIME: 20 MINUTES ■ **START TO FINISH: 35 MINUTES**
36 APPETIZERS

36 large fresh mushrooms (about 2 lb)

1 lb bulk pork sausage

¼ cup freeze-dried chopped chives

2 tablespoons chopped onion

1 clove garlic, finely chopped

¾ cup Original Bisquick mix

¼ cup Italian-style dry bread crumbs

¼ cup grated Parmesan cheese

1 Heat oven to 350°F. Remove stems from mushrooms; finely chop stems.

2 In 10-inch skillet, cook sausage, chopped mushroom stems, chives, onion and garlic until sausage is no longer pink; drain, reserving drippings. Stir Bisquick mix and bread crumbs into sausage mixture until mixture holds together. (If mixture is dry, add 1 to 2 tablespoons reserved drippings.)

3 Spoon about 1 rounded tablespoon sausage mixture into each mushroom cap. In ungreased 15 × 10 × 1-inch pan, place filled mushrooms; sprinkle with cheese.

4 Bake about 15 minutes or until hot. Serve immediately.

High Altitude (3500-6500 ft): No change.

1 APPETIZER: Calories 45 (Calories from Fat 20); Total Fat 2.5g (Saturated Fat 1g); Cholesterol 5mg; Sodium 100mg; Total Carbohydrate 3g (Dietary Fiber 0g); Protein 2g

Smoked Salmon Mini Tarts

PREP TIME: 15 MINUTES ■ **START TO FINISH: 40 MINUTES**

24 APPETIZERS

½ cup Original Bisquick mix

½ cup milk

¼ cup sour cream

½ teaspoon Worcestershire sauce

2 eggs

⅔ cup shredded Cheddar cheese (3 oz)

⅓ cup chopped smoked salmon

2 tablespoons sliced green onions (2 medium)

1 Heat oven to 400°F. Spray 24 mini muffin cups with cooking spray. In small bowl, stir Bisquick mix, milk, sour cream, Worcestershire sauce and eggs with wire whisk or fork until blended. Stir in remaining ingredients. Spoon about 1 tablespoon mixture into each muffin cup.

2 Bake 15 to 20 minutes or until golden brown. Cool 5 minutes. Loosen sides of tarts from pan; remove from pan. Serve warm.

High Altitude (3500-6500 ft): Bake 17 to 22 minutes.

1 APPETIZER: Calories 40 (Calories from Fat 20); Total Fat 2.5g (Saturated Fat 1.5g); Cholesterol 25mg; Sodium 75mg; Total Carbohydrate 2g (Dietary Fiber 0g); Protein 2g

Ham and String Cheese Roll-Ups

PREP TIME: 15 MINUTES ■ **START TO FINISH: 45 MINUTES**
4 SANDWICHES

2 cups Original Bisquick mix

¼ cup water

1 egg

2 teaspoons honey mustard

4 sticks (1 oz each) mozzarella
string cheese

8 slices (about 1 oz each) thinly
sliced cooked ham (from
deli)

1 tablespoon milk

1 Heat oven to 375°F. In medium bowl, stir Bisquick mix, water and egg until dough forms. On surface sprinkled with Bisquick mix, knead dough about 10 times. Divide dough in fourths.

2 For each sandwich, place piece of dough on surface sprinkled with Bisquick mix; roll in Bisquick mix to coat. Press or roll into 6½ × 4½-inch rectangle, ¼ inch thick.

3 Spread each dough rectangle with ½ teaspoon mustard. Wrap each cheese stick with 2 slices ham. Place ham and cheese bundle lengthwise in center of dough. Bring dough up over bundle; pinch to seal. Pinch ends and tuck under. On ungreased cookie sheet, place rolls seam side down. Brush with milk.

4 Bake 18 to 23 minutes or until crust is golden brown. Let stand 5 minutes before serving.

High Altitude (3500–6500 ft): Bake 23 to 28 minutes.

1 SANDWICH: Calories 320 (Calories from Fat 90); Total Fat 10g (Saturated Fat 3g); Cholesterol 75mg; Sodium 1080mg; Total Carbohydrate 42g (Dietary Fiber 0g); Protein 16g

Garlic and Parmesan Churros

PREP TIME: 35 MINUTES ■ **START TO FINISH: 35 MINUTES**
26 APPETIZERS

Vegetable oil for deep frying
1²/₃ cups Original Bisquick mix
1 teaspoon garlic powder
²/₃ cup hot water
½ cup grated Parmesan cheese

1 In 3-quart saucepan, heat 2 to 3 inches oil over medium-high heat to 350°F.

2 In medium bowl, stir Bisquick mix, garlic powder and hot water until soft dough forms. Spoon mixture into decorating bag fitted with star tip #4.

3 Squeeze 5 or 6 (2½-inch) strips of dough at a time into hot oil. If necessary, cut dough with knife or scissors between each churro. Fry 30 seconds to 1 minute 30 seconds, turning frequently, until golden brown. Remove from oil; drain on paper towels. Immediately roll in cheese. Serve warm.

High Altitude (3500–6500 ft): No change.

1 APPETIZER: Calories 160 (Calories from Fat 130); Total Fat 14g (Saturated Fat 2.5g); Cholesterol 0mg; Sodium 125mg; Total Carbohydrate 5g (Dietary Fiber 0g); Protein 1g

Apricot-Glazed Coconut-Chicken Bites

PREP TIME: 15 MINUTES ▪ START TO FINISH: 50 MINUTES
ABOUT 3 DOZEN APPETIZERS

CHICKEN BITES

1/2 cup sweetened condensed milk

2 tablespoons Dijon mustard

1 1/2 cups Original Bisquick mix

2/3 cup flaked coconut

1/2 teaspoon salt

1/2 teaspoon paprika

1 lb boneless skinless chicken breasts, cut into 1-inch pieces

1/4 cup butter or margarine, melted

Hot mustard, if desired

APRICOT GLAZE

1/2 cup apricot spreadable fruit

2 tablespoons honey

2 tablespoons Dijon mustard

1 tablespoon white vinegar

1 Heat oven to 425°F. Mix milk and Dijon mustard. Mix Bisquick mix, coconut, salt and paprika. Dip chicken into milk mixture, then coat with Bisquick mix.

2 Pour 2 tablespoons of the melted butter in a 15 × 10 × 1-inch pan. Place coated chicken in pan. Drizzle remaining butter over chicken.

3 Bake uncovered 20 minutes. Meanwhile, stir all glaze ingredients until blended. Turn chicken; brush with glaze. Bake 10 to 15 minutes longer or until juice or chicken is clear when center of thickest part is cut (170°F) and glaze is bubbly. Serve with hot mustard.

High Altitude (3500-6500 ft): No change.

1 APPETIZER: Calories 80 (Calories from Fat 25); Total Fat 3g (Saturated Fat 1g); Cholesterol 5mg; Sodium 160mg; Total Carbohydrate 10g (Dietary Fiber 0g); Protein 3g

String Cheese Sticks

PREP TIME: 10 MINUTES ■ **START TO FINISH: 20 MINUTES**

8 CHEESE STICKS

2¼ cups Original Bisquick mix

⅔ cup milk

1 package (8 oz) smoked string cheese

1 tablespoon butter or margarine, melted

¼ teaspoon garlic powder

1 can (8 oz) pizza sauce, heated

1 Heat oven to 450°F. In medium bowl, stir Bisquick mix and milk until soft dough forms; beat 30 seconds. Place dough on surface sprinkled with Bisquick mix; gently roll in Bisquick mix to coat. Shape into a ball; knead 10 times.

2 Roll dough ¼ inch thick. Cut into eight 6 × 2-inch rectangles. Roll each rectangle around 1 piece of cheese. Pinch edge into roll to seal; seal ends. Roll on surface to completely enclose cheese sticks. On ungreased cookie sheet, place seam sides down.

3 Bake 8 to 10 minutes or until golden brown. In 1-quart saucepan, mix butter and garlic powder; brush over warm cheese sticks before removing from cookie sheet. Serve warm with pizza sauce for dipping.

High Altitude (3500–6500 ft): Bake 10 to 12 minutes.

1 STICK: Calories 255 (Calories from Fat 110); Total Fat 12g (Saturated Fat 2g); Cholesterol 5mg; Sodium 810mg; Total Carbohydrate 25g (Dietary Fiber 1g); Protein 11g

Beer-Battered Onion Rings with Cajun Dipping Sauce

PREP TIME: 10 MINUTES ■ **START TO FINISH: 20 MINUTES**
5 SERVINGS

ONION RINGS

Vegetable oil for deep frying

1 medium sweet onion (Vidalia or Texas), sliced, separated into rings

2¼ cups Original Bisquick mix

1 cup regular or nonalcoholic beer

1 teaspoon salt

2 eggs

CAJUN DIPPING SAUCE

½ cup mayonnaise or salad dressing

½ cup sour cream

¼ cup chili sauce

1 teaspoon prepared horseradish

¼ teaspoon ground red pepper (cayenne)

1 In deep fryer or heavy 3-quart saucepan, heat 1½ inches oil to 375°F. Toss onion rings and ¼ cup of the Bisquick mix.

2 Stir remaining 2 cups Bisquick mix, the beer, salt and eggs until smooth. (If batter is too thick, stir in additional beer, 1 tablespoon at a time, until desired consistency.) Dip onion rings, a few at a time, into batter, letting excess drip into bowl.

3 Fry about 2 minutes, turning with fork after 1 minute, until golden brown; drain on paper towels.

4 Stir all sauce ingredients until blended. Serve onion rings hot with dipping sauce.

High Altitude (3500-6500 ft): No change.

1 SERVING: Calories 465 (Calories from Fat 305); Total Fat 34g (Saturated Fat 8g); Cholesterol 90mg; Sodium 1270mg; Total Carbohydrate 35g (Dietary Fiber 1g); Protein 6g

Pepperoni-Cheese Breadsticks

PREP TIME: 15 MINUTES ▪ START TO FINISH: 35 MINUTES
ABOUT 20 BREAKSTICKS

2³/₄ cups Original Bisquick mix

1 cup shredded Monterey Jack
cheese (4 oz)

1 medium onion, finely chopped

¹/₂ cup sour cream

¹/₂ cup buttermilk

1 clove garlic, finely chopped

1 package (3 oz) sliced pepperoni, chopped

1 cup grated Parmesan cheese

1 Heat oven to 375°F. Grease 2 cookie sheets. Stir all ingredients except Parmesan cheese until dough forms.

2 Drop dough by heaping tablespoonfuls into Parmesan cheese. Roll in cheese to coat. Roll into 8-inch breadsticks. Place about 1½ inches apart on cookie sheets.

3 Bake 15 to 18 minutes or until golden brown.

High Altitude (3500–6500 ft): No change.

1 BREADSTICK: Calories 150 (Calories from Fat 80); Total Fat 9g (Saturated Fat 4g); Cholesterol 15mg; Sodium 450mg; Total Carbohydrate 11g (Dietary Fiber 0g); Protein 6g

Cheese-Garlic Biscuits

PREP TIME: 10 MINUTES ▪ **START TO FINISH: 20 MINUTES**
9 BISCUITS

2 cups Original Bisquick mix

$\frac{1}{2}$ cup shredded Cheddar
cheese (2 oz)

$\frac{2}{3}$ cup milk

2 tablespoons butter or
margarine, melted

$\frac{1}{8}$ teaspoon garlic powder

1 Heat oven to 450°F. In medium bowl, stir Bisquick mix, cheese and milk until soft dough forms. On ungreased cookie sheet, drop dough by spoonfuls.

2 Bake 8 to 10 minutes or until golden brown. In small bowl, mix butter and garlic powder. Brush over warm biscuits. Serve warm.

High Altitude (3500–6500 ft): No change.

1 BISCUIT: Calories 160 (Calories from Fat 70); Total Fat 8g (Saturated Fat 4g); Cholesterol 15mg; Sodium 390mg; Total Carbohydrate 18g (Dietary Fiber 0g); Protein 4g

Green Chile Cornbread

PREP TIME: 10 MINUTES ■ START TO FINISH: 45 MINUTES
16 SERVINGS

1 cup Original Bisquick mix

1 cup cornmeal

2 tablespoons sugar, if desired

½ teaspoon salt

1 cup milk

¼ cup vegetable oil

2 eggs

1 cup shredded sharp Cheddar cheese (4 oz)

⅔ cup frozen whole kernel corn (from 1-lb bag), thawed, drained

2 tablespoons chopped green chiles (from 4.5-oz can)

1 Heat oven to 400°F. Spray bottom only of 9-inch square pan with cooking spray. In medium bowl, stir Bisquick mix, cornmeal, sugar, salt, milk, oil and eggs with wire whisk or fork just until moistened. Gently stir in remaining ingredients. Pour into pan.

2 Bake 28 to 32 minutes or until light golden brown. Serve warm.

High Altitude (3500–6500 ft): No change.

1 SERVING: Calories 140 (Calories from Fat 70); Total Fat 8g (Saturated Fat 2.5g); Cholesterol 35mg; Sodium 230mg; Total Carbohydrate 14g (Dietary Fiber 0g); Protein 5g

Triple Cheese Flatbread

PREP TIME: 20 MINUTES ■ START TO FINISH: 30 MINUTES
16 SERVINGS

2 cups Original Bisquick mix

½ cup hot water

2 tablespoons butter or margarine, melted

¼ cup shredded Cheddar cheese (1 oz)

¼ cup shredded Monterey Jack cheese (1 oz)

¼ cup grated Parmesan cheese

½ teaspoon garlic powder

½ teaspoon Italian seasoning, if desired

1 Heat oven to 450°F. Mix Bisquick mix and hot water until stiff dough forms. Let stand 10 minutes. Place dough on surface sprinkled with Bisquick mix; gently roll in Bisquick mix to coat. Shape into a ball; knead 60 times.

2 On ungreased cookie sheet, roll or pat dough into 12-inch square. Spread butter over dough. Mix remaining ingredients; sprinkle over dough.

3 Bake 10 to 12 minutes or until edges are golden brown. Serve warm.

High Altitude (3500–6500 ft): No change.

1 SERVING: Calories 90 (Calories from Fat 45); Total Fat 5g (Saturated Fat 2g); Cholesterol 5mg; Sodium 280mg; Total Carbohydrate 9g (Dietary Fiber 0g); Protein 2g

Cornbread Sticks

PREP TIME: 10 MINUTES ● **START TO FINISH: 25 MINUTES**
16 CORNBREAD STICKS

1 cup Original Bisquick mix

1 cup yellow cornmeal

1½ cups buttermilk

2 tablespoons vegetable oil

2 eggs

About 2 tablespoons yellow
    cornmeal

1 Heat oven to 450°F. Grease two 9 × 5-inch loaf pans.

2 In large bowl, stir Bisquick mix, 1 cup cornmeal, the buttermilk, oil and eggs until blended. Pour into pans. Sprinkle with 2 tablespoons cornmeal.

3 Bake about 15 minutes or until toothpick inserted in center comes out clean. Remove from pans. Cut each loaf crosswise into 8 sticks.

High Altitude (3500-6500 ft): Bake about 20 minutes.

1 STICK: Calories 95 (Calories from Fat 35); Total Fat 4g (Saturated Fat 1g); Cholesterol 30mg; Sodium 130mg; Total Carbohydrate 13g (Dietary Fiber 1g); Protein 3g

CHAPTER 3

30-Minute
Meals

Beef and Onion Soup
with Cheesy Biscuit Croutons

PREP TIME: 25 MINUTES ■ START TO FINISH: 30 MINUTES
4 SERVINGS

SOUP

1 lb lean (at least 80%) ground beef

1 envelope onion soup and dip mix (from 2-oz box)

¼ teaspoon pepper

1 can (14 oz) beef broth

3 cups water

1 tablespoon packed brown sugar

1 tablespoon Worcestershire sauce

CROUTONS

1 cup Original Bisquick mix

3 tablespoons grated Parmesan cheese

¼ cup water

¾ cup finely shredded Swiss cheese (3 oz)

1 In 3-quart saucepan, cook beef, onion soup mix and pepper over medium-high heat 5 to 7 minutes, stirring occasionally, until beef is thoroughly cooked; drain. Add broth, water, brown sugar and Worcestershire sauce. Heat to boiling. Reduce heat to medium-low; cook uncovered 10 minutes. Cover; remove from heat.

2 Meanwhile, heat oven to 425°F. Spray cookie sheet with cooking spray. In medium bowl, stir Bisquick mix, Parmesan cheese and water until soft dough forms. Place dough on surface sprinkled with Bisquick mix; roll in Bisquick mix to coat. Shape into a ball; knead 10 times. Press or roll dough into 12 × 6-inch rectangle, ¼ inch thick, on cookie sheet. Cut into 8 squares, but do not separate. Bake 6 to 8 minutes or until golden brown. Remove from oven.

3 Set oven control to broil. Sprinkle croutons with Swiss cheese. Cut and separate squares slightly. Broil with tops 4 to 6 inches from heat 2 to 3 minutes or until cheese is bubbly and slightly browned.

4 Float 1 or 2 croutons in individual bowls of soup. Serve any remaining croutons with soup.

High Altitude (3500–6500 ft): No change.

1 SERVING: Calories 460 (Calories from Fat 220); Total Fat 24g (Saturated Fat 11g); Cholesterol 95mg; Sodium 1630mg; Total Carbohydrate 30g (Dietary Fiber 1g); Protein 31g

Beef and Peppers with Cheese Biscuits

PREP TIME: 20 MINUTES ▪ **START TO FINISH: 30 MINUTES**
6 SERVINGS

1³/₄ cups Original Bisquick mix

¹/₂ cup milk

¹/₂ cup shredded Swiss or
   provolone cheese (2 oz)

1 can (10.75 oz) condensed
   French onion soup

2 packages (5 oz each)
   deli-style sliced cooked beef,
   cut into thin strips

2 small bell peppers, sliced

¹/₂ teaspoon garlic-pepper blend

1¹/₃ cups water

¹/₃ cup all-purpose flour

1 Heat oven to 450°F. In medium bowl, stir Bisquick mix, milk and cheese until soft dough forms; beat 20 strokes. Place dough on surface generously sprinkled with Bisquick mix; gently roll in Bisquick mix to coat. Shape into a ball; knead 10 times.

2 Press or roll dough until ¼ inch thick. With 3-inch round cutter, cut into 6 biscuits. On ungreased cookie sheet, place biscuits.

3 Bake 6 to 8 minutes or until golden brown.

4 Meanwhile, in 2-quart saucepan, mix soup, beef, bell peppers, garlic-pepper blend and 1 cup of the water. Heat to boiling over medium-high heat. Reduce heat to medium-low. In small bowl, stir remaining ⅓ cup water and the flour until mixed; stir into beef mixture. Heat to boiling, stirring frequently, until thickened.

5 Split biscuits. Serve beef mixture over biscuits.

High Altitude (3500–6500 ft): No change.

1 SERVING: Calories 300 (Calories from Fat 90); Total Fat 10g (Saturated Fat 4g); Cholesterol 35mg; Sodium 1340mg; Total Carbohydrate 36g (Dietary Fiber 2g); Protein 17g

Chicken Cutlets
with Creamy Mushroom Gravy

PREP TIME: 30 MINUTES ■ **START TO FINISH: 30 MINUTES**
4 SERVINGS

4 boneless skinless chicken breasts (about 4 oz each)

½ cup Original Bisquick mix

½ teaspoon garlic powder

1 egg

3 tablespoons vegetable oil

1½ cups sliced fresh mushrooms

3 tablespoons Original Bisquick mix

2 medium green onions, sliced (2 tablespoons)

1 cup milk

1½ teaspoons soy sauce

1 Between pieces of plastic wrap or waxed paper, place each chicken breast smooth side down; gently pound with flat side of meat mallet or rolling pin until about ¼ inch thick.

2 In shallow dish, stir ½ cup Bisquick mix and the garlic powder. In another shallow dish, beat egg. Dip chicken in egg, then coat with Bisquick mixture.

3 In 12-inch nonstick skillet, heat 2 tablespoons of the oil over medium heat. Add chicken. Cook about 3 minutes or until golden brown. Turn chicken; cover and cook 4 to 6 minutes longer or until chicken is no longer pink in center. Remove to serving platter; cover to keep warm.

4 In same skillet, heat remaining 1 tablespoon oil over medium heat. Add mushrooms; cook 3 to 4 minutes, stirring frequently, until browned. Add 3 tablespoons Bisquick mix and the onions; cook and stir until mixed. Stir in milk and soy sauce. Cook until mixture is thick and bubbly. Serve over chicken.

High Altitude (3500-6500 ft): For gravy, add an additional 2 tablespoons milk and cook 3 to 4 minutes.

1 SERVING: Calories 370 (Calories from Fat 170); Total Fat 19g (Saturated Fat 4.5g); Cholesterol 125mg; Sodium 470mg; Total Carbohydrate 18g (Dietary Fiber 0g); Protein 31g

Buffalo-Style Chicken Nuggets

PREP TIME: 10 MINUTES ▪ **START TO FINISH: 25 MINUTES**
4 SERVINGS

1½ cups Corn Chex® cereal

½ cup Original Bisquick mix

2 teaspoons paprika

¼ teaspoon seasoned salt

¼ teaspoon ground red pepper (cayenne)

1 tablespoon canola or soybean oil

1 teaspoon red pepper sauce or hot sauce

1 lb boneless skinless chicken breasts, cut into 2-inch pieces

¼ cup fat-free sour cream

¼ cup reduced-fat ranch dressing

1 Heat oven to 425°F. Place cereal in 1-gallon resealable food-storage plastic bag; crush with rolling pin. Add Bisquick mix, paprika, seasoned salt and red pepper to cereal; mix well.

2 In small bowl, mix oil and red pepper sauce. Coat chicken pieces with oil mixture.

3 In bag of cereal mixture, shake about 6 chicken pieces at a time until coated. Shake off any extra mixture. On ungreased cookie sheet, place chicken pieces in single layer.

4 Bake about 10 minutes or until chicken is no longer pink in center. Meanwhile, in small bowl, mix sour cream and dressing. Serve sauce with chicken.

High Altitude (3500–6500 ft): Bake about 15 minutes.

1 SERVING: Calories 320 (Calories from Fat 110); Total Fat 12g (Saturated Fat 2g); Cholesterol 75mg; Sodium 640mg; Total Carbohydrate 25g (Dietary Fiber 1g); Protein 28g

Easy Turkey Club Bake

PREP TIME: 10 MINUTES ▪ **START TO FINISH: 30 MINUTES**
6 SERVINGS

2 cups Original Bisquick mix

⅓ cup mayonnaise or salad dressing

⅓ cup milk

2 cups cubed cooked turkey

2 tablespoons sliced green onions (2 medium)

6 slices bacon, crisply cooked, crumbled

¼ cup mayonnaise or salad dressing

1 large tomato, chopped (1 cup)

1 cup shredded Colby-Monterey Jack cheese (4 oz)

1 Heat oven to 450°F. Spray cookie sheet with cooking spray. In medium bowl, stir Bisquick mix, ⅓ cup mayonnaise and the milk until soft dough forms. On cookie sheet, press dough into 12 × 8-inch rectangle.

2 Bake 8 to 10 minutes or until crust is golden brown.

3 In medium bowl, mix turkey, onions, bacon and ¼ cup mayonnaise. Spoon over crust to within ¼ inch of edges. Sprinkle with tomato and cheese.

4 Bake about 5 minutes or until mixture is hot and cheese is melted.

High Altitude (3500–6500 ft): In step 2, bake crust about 10 minutes. In step 4, bake 6 to 8 minutes.

1 SERVING: Calories 530 (Calories from Fat 310); Total Fat 35g (Saturated Fat 10g); Cholesterol 75mg; Sodium 950mg; Total Carbohydrate 29g (Dietary Fiber 1g); Protein 25g

Barbecue Pork Shortcakes

PREP TIME: 10 MINUTES ■ **START TO FINISH: 20 MINUTES**
4 SANDWICHES

½ cup milk

2 teaspoons maple extract

1¾ cups Original Bisquick mix

1 container (18 oz) refrigerated fully cooked original barbecue sauce with shredded pork

1 cup frozen mixed vegetables, thawed, drained

2 tablespoons maple-flavored syrup

1 Heat oven to 450°F. In large bowl, mix milk and maple extract. Stir in Bisquick mix until soft dough forms; beat 20 strokes.

2 Place dough on surface generously sprinkled with Bisquick mix; gently roll in Bisquick mix to coat. Shape into a ball; knead 10 times. Press or roll into 6-inch square, about ½ inch thick. Cut into 4 square biscuits. On ungreased cookie sheet, place biscuits.

3 Bake 7 to 9 minutes or until lightly browned.

4 Meanwhile, place pork in 1½-quart microwavable bowl. Cover with microwavable plastic wrap, folding back one edge ¼ inch to vent steam. Microwave on High 2 minutes; stir. If not hot, cover and microwave up to 4 minutes longer, stirring every minute. Stir in vegetables and maple syrup. Cover and microwave on High 1 minute.

5 To serve, split biscuits in half. Fill with pork mixture.

High Altitude (3500–6500 ft): No change.

1 SANDWICH: Calories 490 (Calories from Fat 110); Total Fat 12g (Saturated Fat 3.5g); Cholesterol 35mg; Sodium 1530mg; Total Carbohydrate 74g (Dietary Fiber 3g); Protein 20g

Coconut Shrimp

PREP TIME: 30 MINUTES ■ **START TO FINISH: 30 MINUTES**
6 SERVINGS

1 lb uncooked deveined peeled medium shrimp (31 to 35), thawed if frozen, tail shells removed

1 cup Original Bisquick mix

¾ cup milk

1 egg

1 cup vegetable oil

2½ cups flaked coconut

½ cup chili sauce

½ cup apricot preserves

1 Pat shrimp dry with paper towels. In medium bowl, stir Bisquick mix, milk and egg with wire whisk or fork until blended. Add shrimp; gently stir to coat well.

2 In 10-inch skillet, heat oil over medium heat to 375°F. In shallow dish, place half of the coconut (add remaining coconut after coating half of the shrimp). Cooking in batches, remove shrimp one at a time from batter and coat with coconut; place in oil in single layer.

3 Cook 3 to 4 minutes, turning once, until coating is crispy and golden brown and shrimp are pink (cut 1 shrimp open to check doneness). Drain on paper towels.

4 In small bowl, mix chili sauce and apricot preserves. Serve shrimp with sauce for dipping.

High Altitude (3500–6500 ft): Cook shrimp 4 to 5 minutes, turning every minute.

1 SERVING: Calories 440 (Calories from Fat 190); Total Fat 21g (Saturated Fat 11g); Cholesterol 110mg; Sodium 520mg; Total Carbohydrate 50g (Dietary Fiber 3g); Protein 15g

Potato Patties with Black Bean Salsa

PREP TIME: 10 MINUTES ■ **START TO FINISH: 25 MINUTES**
6 SERVINGS

1 bag (1 lb 4 oz) refrigerated Southwest-style shredded hash brown potatoes

1 cup shredded reduced-fat Cheddar cheese (4 oz)

½ cup Original Bisquick mix

3 eggs, beaten, or ¾ cup fat-free egg product

¼ cup canola or olive oil

1 can (11 oz) whole kernel corn with red and green peppers, drained

1 can (15 oz) black beans, drained, rinsed

¼ cup chunky-style salsa

1 In large bowl, mix potatoes, cheese, Bisquick mix and eggs until blended.

2 In 12-inch skillet, heat 2 tablespoons of the oil over medium heat. For each patty, spoon about ½ cup potato mixture into oil in skillet. Flatten with back of spatula.

3 Cook patties about 4 minutes, turning once, until golden brown. Remove from skillet; cover to keep warm while cooking remaining patties. Add remaining 2 tablespoons oil as needed to prevent sticking.

4 In 2-quart saucepan, heat corn, beans and salsa over medium heat 2 to 3 minutes, stirring occasionally, until hot. Serve over patties.

High Altitude (3500–6500 ft): In step 4, increase cook time to 4 to 5 minutes.

1 SERVING: Calories 400 (Calories from Fat 140); Total Fat 15g (Saturated Fat 3g); Cholesterol 110mg; Sodium 430mg; Total Carbohydrate 50g (Dietary Fiber 10g); Protein 17g

Curried Country Chicken

PREP TIME: 15 MINUTES ▫ **START TO FINISH: 30 MINUTES**
2 SERVINGS

2 boneless skinless chicken breasts (about ½ lb), cut into 1-inch pieces

¼ cup chopped onion (½ medium)

¼ cup chopped green bell pepper

1 can (14.5 oz) diced tomatoes, undrained

¼ cup golden raisins

½ to 1 teaspoon curry powder

⅛ teaspoon salt

⅛ teaspoon ground nutmeg

⅔ cup Bisquick Heart Smart mix

3 tablespoons cornmeal

⅓ cup fat-free (skim) milk

1 In 3-quart nonstick saucepan, cook chicken over medium-high heat 3 minutes, stirring occasionally, until no longer pink in center. Stir in onion and bell pepper. Cook about 2 minutes, stirring occasionally, until vegetables are tender.

2 Stir in tomatoes, raisins, curry powder, salt and nutmeg. Heat to boiling.

3 Meanwhile, in small bowl, stir Bisquick mix, cornmeal and milk until soft dough forms.

4 Drop dough by 4 spoonfuls onto hot chicken mixture. Reduce heat to medium-low. Cover; cook 10 to 12 minutes or until dumplings are dry.

High Altitude (3500–6500 ft): In step 2, add ¼ cup water with tomatoes. In step 4, cook covered 11 to 13 minutes.

1 SERVING: Calories 450 (Calories from Fat 60); Total Fat 7g (Saturated Fat 1g); Cholesterol 70mg; Sodium 920mg; Total Carbohydrate 65g (Dietary Fiber 4g); Protein 33g

Southwest Country Chicken: Omit raisins, curry powder and nutmeg. Add 1 to 2 teaspoons chili powder with the tomatoes.

Cajun Country Chicken: Omit raisins, curry powder and nutmeg. Add 1 teaspoon Cajun seasoning and ¼ teaspoon dried oregano leaves with the tomatoes.

Herbed Fish

PREP TIME: 15 MINUTES ▪ **START TO FINISH: 15 MINUTES**
2 SERVINGS

½ lb cod or other mild-flavored fish fillets, about ½ inch thick

¼ cup Bisquick Heart Smart mix

2 tablespoons garlic herb dry bread crumbs

1½ teaspoons chopped fresh or ½ teaspoon dried basil leaves

⅛ teaspoon salt

2 tablespoons fat-free egg product or 1 egg white

1 tablespoon olive or vegetable oil

1 Cut fish into 2 serving pieces. In small shallow dish, stir Bisquick mix, bread crumbs, basil and salt. In another shallow dish, beat egg white.

2 In 8-inch skillet, heat oil over medium heat. Dip fish into egg white, then coat with Bisquick mixture.

3 Reduce heat to medium-low. Cook fish in oil 8 to 10 minutes, turning once, until fish flakes easily with fork and is brown on both sides.

High Altitude (3500–6500 ft): No change.

1 SERVING: Calories 250 (Calories from Fat 90); Total Fat 9g (Saturated Fat 1.5g); Cholesterol 60mg; Sodium 560mg; Total Carbohydrate 15g (Dietary Fiber 0g); Protein 25g

Mini Barbecued Meat Loaves

PREP TIME: 10 MINUTES ▪ START TO FINISH: 30 MINUTES
6 SERVINGS

½ cup barbecue sauce

1 lb lean (at least 80%) ground beef

½ lb ground pork

½ cup Original Bisquick mix

¼ teaspoon pepper

1 small onion, finely chopped (¼ cup)

1 egg

1 Heat oven to 450°F.

2 Reserve ¼ cup of the barbecue sauce. Mix remaining ingredients and ¼ cup barbecue sauce. Place meat mixture in ungreased 13 × 9-inch pan; pat into 12 × 4-inch rectangle. Cut lengthwise down center and then crosswise into sixths to form 12 loaves. Separate loaves slightly. Brush loaves with reserved ¼ cup barbecue sauce.

3 Bake 18 to 22 minutes or until loaves are no longer pink in the center, juice is clear and meat thermometer reads 160° when inserted in center of loaves.

High Altitude (3500-6500 ft): No change.

1 SERVING: Calories 305 (Calories from Fat 160); Total Fat 18g (Saturated Fat 7g); Cholesterol 100mg; Sodium 410mg; Total Carbohydrate 14g (Dietary Fiber 0g); Protein 22g

CHAPTER 4

Effortless

Dinners

Very Veggie Pizza Pie

PREP TIME: 15 MINUTES ▪ **START TO FINISH: 40 MINUTES**
8 SERVINGS

1 package (8 oz) sliced
    mushrooms (3 cups)

1 small zucchini, sliced (1 cup)

1 medium bell pepper, sliced

1 clove garlic, finely chopped

2 cups Bisquick Heart
    Smart mix

1/4 cup process cheese sauce or
    spread (room temperature)

1/4 cup very hot water

1/2 cup pizza sauce

3/4 cup shredded reduced-fat
    mozzarella cheese (3 oz)

1 Heat oven to 375°F. Spray cookie sheet with cooking spray. Spray 10-inch skillet with cooking spray; heat over medium-high heat. In skillet, cook mushrooms, zucchini, bell pepper and garlic about 5 minutes, stirring occasionally, until vegetables are crisp-tender.

2 In medium bowl, stir Bisquick mix, cheese sauce and hot water until soft dough forms. Place dough on surface sprinkled with Bisquick mix; roll in Bisquick mix to coat. Shape into a ball; knead about 5 times or until smooth. Roll or pat dough into 14-inch circle on cookie sheet. Spread pizza sauce over dough to within 3 inches of edge. Top with vegetable mixture. Sprinkle with cheese. Fold edge of dough over mixture.

3 Bake 23 to 25 minutes or until crust is golden brown and cheese is bubbly.

High Altitude (3500–6500 ft): Heat oven to 400°F. Use 1/3 cup very hot water.

1 SERVING: Calories 170 (Calories from Fat 55); Total Fat 6g (Saturated Fat 2g); Cholesterol 10mg; Sodium 490mg; Total Carbohydrate 24g (Dietary Fiber 2g); Protein 7g

Stuffed Pizza

PREP TIME: 30 MINUTES ▪ **START TO FINISH: 55 MINUTES**
8 SERVINGS

½ lb bulk Italian pork sausage

½ lb lean (at least 80%) ground beef

3⅓ cups Original Bisquick mix

¾ cup cold water

3 cups shredded mozzarella cheese (12 oz)

1 jar or can (14 to 15 oz) pizza sauce

1 cup sliced fresh mushrooms (3 oz)

¼ cup chopped green bell pepper

1 Heat oven to 450°F. Spray 13 × 9-inch (3-quart) glass baking dish with cooking spray. In 10-inch skillet, cook sausage and ground beef over medium-high heat 5 to 7 minutes, stirring frequently, until thoroughly cooked; drain. Set aside.

2 In large bowl, stir Bisquick mix and cold water until dough forms. Divide dough into 2 parts, 1 part slightly larger. Press or roll larger part of dough into 16 × 14-inch rectangle on surface sprinkled with Bisquick mix. Fold crosswise into thirds. Place in center of baking dish; unfold. Press on bottom and up sides of dish. Sprinkle with 1 cup of the cheese; top with ¾ cup of the pizza sauce, the meat mixture, mushrooms and bell pepper and 1½ cups of the cheese.

3 Press or roll remaining part of dough into 13 × 9-inch rectangle. Fold crosswise into thirds. Place on cheese in center of baking dish; unfold. Press bottom and top crust edges together to seal. Make small slits in top crust. Spread remaining pizza sauce over crust; sprinkle with remaining cheese.

4 Bake uncovered 22 to 25 minutes or until edges of crust are golden brown.

High Altitude (3500–6500 ft): In step 3, do not sprinkle remaining cheese on pizza before baking. Bake pizza uncovered 25 minutes. Sprinkle with remaining cheese; bake 3 to 5 minutes longer to melt cheese.

1 SERVING: Calories 450 (Calories from Fat 200); Total Fat 22g (Saturated Fat 10g); Cholesterol 50mg; Sodium 1190mg; Total Carbohydrate 39g (Dietary Fiber 2g); Protein 24g

Pizza Biscuit Bake

PREP TIME: 15 MINUTES ■ **START TO FINISH: 40 MINUTES**

8 SERVINGS

3⅓ cups Original Bisquick mix

1 cup milk

2 cans (8 oz each) pizza sauce

1 package (8 oz) sliced pepperoni

2 cups shredded mozzarella cheese (8 oz)

1 Heat oven to 375°F. Spray 13 × 9-inch (3-quart) glass baking dish with cooking spray. In medium bowl, stir Bisquick mix and milk until soft dough forms.

2 Drop half of dough by spoonfuls evenly over bottom of baking dish (dough will not completely cover bottom of dish). Drizzle 1 can pizza sauce over dough. Scatter half of the pepperoni over sauce. Top with 1 cup of the cheese. Repeat layers with remaining dough, pizza sauce, pepperoni and cheese.

3 Bake 20 to 25 minutes or until golden brown.

High Altitude (3500–6500 ft): Bake 25 to 30 minutes.

1 SERVING: Calories 450 (Calories from Fat 220); Total Fat 24g (Saturated Fat 10g); Cholesterol 50mg; Sodium 1530mg; Total Carbohydrate 41g (Dietary Fiber 2g); Protein 19g

owboy Barbecue Chicken Pizza

PREP TIME: 15 MINUTES ▪ START TO FINISH: 40 MINUTES
8 SERVINGS

2 cups Original Bisquick mix

¼ cup sour cream

¼ cup very hot water

3 cups cubed cooked chicken

1 cup barbecue sauce

4 medium green onions, sliced (¼ cup)

¼ cup chopped packaged precooked bacon (about 4 slices from 2.2-oz package)

1½ cups shredded Colby-Monterey Jack cheese (6 oz)

1 Heat oven to 400°F. In medium bowl, stir Bisquick mix, sour cream and hot water until soft dough forms.

2 On surface sprinkled with Bisquick mix, shape dough into a ball. Knead 5 times. Roll dough into 14-inch round; fold round in half. Place dough on ungreased 14-inch pizza pan or large cookie sheet; unfold dough.

3 In medium bowl, mix chicken, barbecue sauce and onions. Spread chicken mixture over dough to within 1 inch of edge. Fold edge just to chicken mixture. Top with half of the bacon. Sprinkle with cheese and remaining bacon.

4 Bake 20 to 25 minutes or until crust is light golden brown and cheese is melted.

High Altitude (3500–6500 ft): Bake 18 to 23 minutes.

1 SERVING: Calories 380 (Calories from Fat 160); Total Fat 17g (Saturated Fat 8g); Cholesterol 75mg; Sodium 920mg; Total Carbohydrate 33g (Dietary Fiber 0g); Protein 23g

Sweet-and-Sour Chicken Stir-Fry

PREP TIME: 30 MINUTES ▪ **START TO FINISH: 30 MINUTES**
6 SERVINGS (1¼ CUPS EACH)

1 cup Original Bisquick mix

½ teaspoon pepper

2 eggs

1 lb boneless skinless chicken breasts, cut into 1-inch cubes

¼ cup vegetable oil

3 medium carrots, cut diagonally into ¼-inch slices (1½ cups)

1 medium green bell pepper, cut into strips (1 cup)

1 small onion, thinly sliced, separated into rings (⅓ cup)

1 can (20 oz) pineapple chunks, drained

½ cup sweet-and-sour sauce

1 In large resealable food-storage plastic bag, mix Bisquick mix and pepper.

2 In medium bowl, beat eggs slightly. Stir in chicken until combined. Using slotted spoon, remove chicken from eggs; place in bag with Bisquick mix. Seal bag; shake bag until chicken is coated.

3 In 12-inch skillet, heat 1 tablespoon of the oil over medium-high heat. Add carrots; cook 2 minutes, stirring frequently. Add bell pepper and onion; cook 2 minutes longer, stirring frequently. Remove from skillet.

4 In same skillet, heat remaining oil. Add chicken; cook, stirring frequently, until golden brown on outside and no longer pink in center. Add vegetables; cook about 2 minutes, stirring frequently, until thoroughly heated. Stir in pineapple and sweet-and-sour sauce; cook until thoroughly heated.

High Altitude (3500–6500 ft): No change.

1 SERVING: Calories 370 (Calories from Fat 150); Total Fat 16g (Saturated Fat 3.5g); Cholesterol 115mg; Sodium 410mg; Total Carbohydrate 34g (Dietary Fiber 3g); Protein 21g

Easy Chicken Pot Pie

PREP TIME: 10 MINUTES ■ **START TO FINISH: 40 MINUTES**
6 SERVINGS

1 bag (1 lb) frozen mixed
  vegetables, thawed, drained

1 cup diced cooked chicken

1 can (10.75 oz) condensed
  cream of chicken soup

1 cup Original Bisquick mix

½ cup milk

1 egg

1 Heat oven to 400°F. In ungreased 2-quart casserole, mix vegetables, chicken and soup until blended.

2 In medium bowl, stir all remaining ingredients with wire whisk or fork until blended. Pour over chicken mixture.

3 Bake uncovered about 30 minutes or until crust is golden brown.

High Altitude (3500–6500 ft): Heat oven to 425°F.

1 SERVING: Calories 240 (Calories from Fat 80); Total Fat 9g (Saturated Fat 3g); Cholesterol 60mg; Sodium 670mg; Total Carbohydrate 28g (Dietary Fiber 4g); Protein 13g

Barbecue Crispy Chicken Melts

PREP TIME: 10 MINUTES ▪ **START TO FINISH: 45 MINUTES**
4 SERVINGS

3 tablespoons butter or margarine

½ cup Original Bisquick mix

¼ teaspoon pepper

¼ cup milk

4 boneless skinless chicken breasts (about 1¼ lb)

¼ cup barbecue sauce

½ cup shredded Cheddar cheese (2 oz)

1 Heat oven to 425°F. In 13 × 9-inch pan, heat butter in oven 2 to 3 minutes or until melted.

2 In shallow dish, stir Bisquick mix and pepper. Pour milk into small bowl. Coat chicken with Bisquick mixture, then dip in milk; coat again with Bisquick mixture. Place in pan.

3 Bake about 30 minutes or until juice of chicken is clear when center of thickest part is cut (170°F).

4 In small microwavable bowl, microwave barbecue sauce uncovered on High about 30 seconds or until warm. Spoon sauce evenly over chicken; top with cheese.

High Altitude (3500–6500 ft): No change.

1 SERVING: Calories 400 (Calories from Fat 180); Total Fat 20g (Saturated Fat 10g); Cholesterol 125mg; Sodium 580mg; Total Carbohydrate 17g (Dietary Fiber 0g); Protein 36g

Italian Chicken Fingers

PREP TIME: 20 MINUTES ◼ **START TO FINISH: 40 MINUTES**
4 SERVINGS

1 egg

1 package (14 oz) uncooked chicken breast tenders (not breaded)

1¼ cups Original Bisquick mix

1 teaspoon Italian seasoning

3 tablespoons butter or margarine, melted

1 cup tomato pasta sauce, heated

1 Heat oven to 450°F. Spray 15 × 10 × 1-inch pan with cooking spray. In medium bowl, beat egg slightly. Add chicken; toss to coat.

2 In resealable food-storage plastic bag, place Bisquick mix and Italian seasoning; seal bag and shake to mix. Add chicken; seal bag and shake to coat chicken with Bisquick mixture. Place chicken in single layer in pan. Drizzle with butter.

3 Bake 14 to 16 minutes, turning chicken after 6 minutes, until chicken is brown and crisp on the outside and no longer pink in center. Serve with pasta sauce for dipping.

High Altitude (3500–6500 ft): No change.

1 SERVING: Calories 410 (Calories from Fat 160); Total Fat 17g (Saturated Fat 8g); Cholesterol 120mg; Sodium 950mg; Total Carbohydrate 36g (Dietary Fiber 2g); Protein 26g

Chicken-Veggie Casserole

PREP TIME: 20 MINUTES ● **START TO FINISH: 45 MINUTES**
6 SERVINGS

1 can (10.75 oz) condensed
    Cheddar cheese soup

1 cup milk

2 tablespoons dried minced
    onion

2 cups frozen mixed vegetables,
    thawed, drained

1½ cups cut-up cooked chicken

2 cups Original Bisquick mix

¼ cup sliced green onions

2 tablespoons mayonnaise or
    salad dressing

1 egg

1 Heat oven to 400°F. In 3-quart saucepan, heat soup, milk and dried minced onion to boiling, stirring constantly. Stir in vegetables and chicken. Pour into ungreased 11 × 7-inch (2-quart) glass baking dish.

2 In medium bowl, mix all remaining ingredients with fork until crumbly. Sprinkle over chicken mixture.

3 Bake uncovered about 25 minutes or until topping is golden brown and soup is bubbly.

High Altitude (3500–6500 ft): Use 13 x 9-inch (3-quart) glass baking dish.

1 SERVING: Calories 400 (Calories from Fat 150); Total Fat 17g (Saturated Fat 5g); Cholesterol 80mg; Sodium 1050mg; Total Carbohydrate 42g (Dietary Fiber 4g); Protein 19g

Alfredo Chicken Bake

PREP TIME: 15 MINUTES ▪ START TO FINISH: 40 MINUTES
4 SERVINGS

1 package (9 oz) frozen diced
   cooked chicken, thawed

½ cup frozen baby sweet peas

½ cup shredded Swiss cheese
   (2 oz)

¾ cup Alfredo pasta sauce

2 tablespoons slivered almonds

1 cup Original Bisquick mix

⅓ cup milk

1 Heat oven to 425°F. In 1½-quart saucepan, heat chicken, peas, cheese, Alfredo sauce and almonds to boiling over medium-high heat. Pour into ungreased 1½-quart casserole.

2 In small bowl, stir Bisquick mix and milk until soft dough forms. Drop dough by about 12 spoonfuls onto chicken mixture.

3 Bake uncovered 20 to 25 minutes or until golden brown.

High Altitude (3500-6500 ft): In step 1, stir ¼ cup water into chicken mixture. In step 3, bake uncovered 25 to 30 minutes.

1 SERVING: Calories 490 (Calories from Fat 260); Total Fat 29g (Saturated Fat 14g); Cholesterol 115mg; Sodium 850mg; Total Carbohydrate 27g (Dietary Fiber 2g); Protein 30g

Parmesan Chicken, Provolone and Ham Bundles

PREP TIME: 15 MINUTES ▪ START TO FINISH: 50 MINUTES
4 SERVINGS

2 cups Original Bisquick mix

½ teaspoon garlic powder

½ cup boiling water

4 slices (¾ oz each) provolone cheese

4 thin slices (about 1 oz each) cooked ham

4 large (about ½ lb) uncooked chicken breast tenders (not breaded)

1 tablespoon butter or margarine, melted

4 teaspoons grated Parmesan cheese

½ cup tomato pasta sauce, heated

1 Heat oven to 375°F (if using dark or nonstick pan, heat oven to 350°F). In medium bowl, stir Bisquick mix, garlic powder and boiling water until dough forms.

2 Divide dough into fourths. Place pieces on surface sprinkled with Bisquick mix; roll in Bisquick mix to coat. Press or roll each piece into 7 × 5-inch rectangle, ¼ inch thick.

3 Center 1 provolone cheese slice and 1 ham slice on each rectangle, folding to fit if needed. Top each with 1 chicken tender. Starting at 7-inch side, roll up each bundle. Press ends and seam to seal. Tuck ends under. On ungreased cookie sheet, place seam side down. Brush with butter; sprinkle with Parmesan cheese.

4 Bake 25 to 33 minutes or until meat thermometer inserted in center of chicken reads 170°F and bundles are golden brown. Serve topped with pasta sauce.

High Altitude (3500–6500 ft): No change.

1 SERVING: Calories 490 (Calories from Fat 180); Total Fat 21g (Saturated Fat 9g); Cholesterol 65mg; Sodium 1620mg; Total Carbohydrate 46g (Dietary Fiber 2g); Protein 30g

Cajun Chicken

PREP TIME: 20 MINUTES ■ START TO FINISH: 20 MINUTES
4 SERVINGS

4 boneless skinless chicken breasts (about 1¼ lb)

1½ cups cornflakes cereal, crushed (½ cup)

½ cup Original Bisquick mix

2 teaspoons Cajun seasoning

½ cup water

2 tablespoons butter or margarine

1 Between pieces of plastic wrap or waxed paper, place each chicken breast smooth side down; gently pound with flat side of meat mallet or rolling pin until about ¼ inch thick.

2 In shallow bowl, mix cereal, Bisquick mix and Cajun seasoning. Dip chicken into water, then coat with cereal mixture.

3 In 12-inch nonstick skillet, melt butter over medium heat. Cook chicken in butter 8 to 10 minutes, turning once, until chicken is no longer pink in center.

High Altitude (3500–6500 ft): Cook chicken 10 to 12 minutes.

1 SERVING: Calories 275 (Calories from Fat 90); Total Fat 10g (Saturated Fat 2g); Cholesterol 75mg; Sodium 450mg; Total Carbohydrate 18g (Dietary Fiber 1g); Protein 28g

Thai Chicken with Spicy Peanut Sauce

PREP TIME: 20 MINUTES ▪ **START TO FINISH: 50 MINUTES**
4 SERVINGS

THAI CHICKEN

3 tablespoons butter or
  margarine

1 cup Original Bisquick mix

1½ teaspoons curry powder

1½ teaspoons garlic powder

1 teaspoon ground ginger

4 boneless skinless chicken
  breasts (about 1¼ lb)

⅓ cup milk

2 tablespoons cocktail peanuts,
  finely chopped

SPICY PEANUT SAUCE

½ cup plain yogurt

¼ cup creamy peanut butter

½ cup milk

1 tablespoon soy sauce

⅛ teaspoon ground red pepper
  (cayenne)

1 Heat oven to 425°F. In 13 × 9-inch pan, melt butter in oven.

2 In large bowl, mix Bisquick mix, curry powder, garlic powder and ginger. Dip chicken into milk, then coat with Bisquick mixture. Place in dish.

3 Bake uncovered 20 minutes; turn chicken. Bake about 10 minutes longer or until juice of chicken is clear when center of thickest part is cut (170°F).

4 Meanwhile, in 10-inch nonstick skillet, mix all peanut sauce ingredients. Cook over medium heat 3 to 4 minutes, stirring occasionally, until mixture begins to thicken. Serve sauce over chicken. Sprinkle with peanuts.

High Altitude (3500–6500 ft): No change.

1 SERVING: Calories 510 (Calories from Fat 260); Total Fat 29g (Saturated Fat 7g); Cholesterol 0mg; Sodium 950mg; Total Carbohydrate 27g (Dietary Fiber 2g); Protein 37g

Turkey and Cornbread Stuffing Casserole

PREP TIME: 10 MINUTES ▪ START TO FINISH: 55 MINUTES
6 SERVINGS

1 can (10¾ oz) condensed
   cream of chicken or
   celery soup

1¼ cups milk

1 cup frozen green peas

½ cup dried cranberries

4 medium green onions,
   sliced (¼ cup)

2 cups cut-up cooked turkey
   or chicken

1½ cups corn bread
   stuffing mix

1 cup Original Bisquick mix

¼ cup milk

2 eggs

1 Heat oven to 400°F. Grease 3-quart casserole. In 3-quart saucepan, heat soup and milk to boiling, stirring frequently. Stir in peas, cranberries and onions. Heat to boiling, stirring frequently; remove from heat. Stir in turkey and stuffing mix. Spoon into casserole.

2 In small bowl, stir remaining ingredients until blended. Pour over stuffing mixture.

3 Bake uncovered 35 to 40 minutes or until knife inserted in center comes out clean.

High Altitude (3500–6500 ft): Use 1½ cups milk instead of 1¼ cups.

1 SERVING: Calories 505 (Calories from Fat 215); Total Fat 24g (Saturated Fat 7g); Cholesterol 150mg; Sodium 1050mg; Total Carbohydrate 53g (Dietary Fiber 6g); Protein 25g

Impossibly Easy Barbecue Chicken Pie

PREP TIME: 10 MINUTES ■ **START TO FINISH: 45 MINUTES**
6 SERVINGS

2 cups cubed cooked chicken

1 cup frozen whole kernel corn, thawed

¼ cup chopped fresh parsley

½ cup Original Bisquick mix

¾ cup milk

¼ cup barbecue sauce

2 eggs

2 tablespoons barbecue sauce

¾ cup French-fried onions

Additional barbecue sauce, if desired

1 Heat oven to 400°F. Spray 9-inch glass pie plate with cooking spray. Layer chicken, corn and 3 tablespoons of the parsley in pie plate.

2 In medium bowl, stir Bisquick mix, milk, ¼ cup barbecue sauce and eggs with wire whisk or fork until blended. Pour into pie plate.

3 Bake 28 to 32 minutes or until knife inserted in center comes out clean. Brush 2 tablespoons barbecue sauce over top of pie. Sprinkle onions evenly over sauce.

4 Bake 2 to 3 minutes longer or until onions are golden brown. Remove from oven; sprinkle with remaining 1 tablespoon parsley. Serve with barbecue sauce, heated.

High Altitude (3500–6500 ft): No change.

1 SERVING: Calories 260 (Calories from Fat 100); Total Fat 11g (Saturated Fat 3g); Cholesterol 115mg; Sodium 420mg; Total Carbohydrate 23g (Dietary Fiber 1g); Protein 18g

Impossibly Easy Barbecue Pork Pie: Substitute 2 cups cubed cooked pork for the chicken.

Impossibly Easy Chicken and Broccoli Pie

PREP TIME: 20 MINUTES ▪ **START TO FINISH: 1 HOUR 5 MINUTES**
6 SERVINGS

1 bag (10 oz) frozen chopped broccoli, thawed, drained

1½ cups shredded Cheddar cheese (6 oz)

1 cup cut-up cooked chicken

1 medium onion, chopped (½ cup)

½ cup Original Bisquick mix

1 cup milk

½ teaspoon salt

¼ teaspoon pepper

2 eggs

1 Heat oven to 400°F. Grease 9-inch glass pie plate. In pie plate, sprinkle broccoli, 1 cup of the cheese, the chicken and onion.

2 In medium bowl, stir remaining ingredients until blended. Pour into pie plate.

3 Bake 30 to 35 minutes or until knife inserted in center comes out clean. Sprinkle with remaining ½ cup cheese. Bake 1 to 2 minutes or until cheese is melted. Let stand 5 minutes before serving.

High Altitude (3500–6500 ft): Heat oven to 425°F. Increase first bake time to 33 to 38 minutes.

1 SERVING: Calories 260 (Calories from Fat 145); Total Fat 16g (Saturated Fat 8g); Cholesterol 125mg; Sodium 580mg; Total Carbohydrate 12g (Dietary Fiber 2g); Protein 19g

X

Very Good

Heart Smart Deluxe Cheeseburger Melt

PREP TIME: 15 MINUTES ▪ START TO FINISH: 45 MINUTES

8 SERVINGS

1⅓ cups Bisquick Heart Smart mix

¼ cup water

½ cup fat-free egg product or 4 egg whites

1½ cups shredded reduced-fat Cheddar cheese (6 oz)

1 lb extra-lean (at least 90%) ground beef

1 can (10.75 oz) condensed 98% fat-free cream of mushroom soup

1 cup frozen mixed vegetables

1 Heat oven to 400°F. Spray 13 × 9-inch pan with cooking spray. In medium bowl, stir Bisquick mix, water, egg product and 1 cup of the cheese. Spread mixture in pan.

2 In 10-inch skillet, cook beef over medium-high heat 5 to 7 minutes, stirring frequently, until thoroughly cooked; drain. Stir in soup and vegetables; heat until hot. Spread over batter in pan.

3 Bake 23 to 25 minutes or until edges are light golden brown. Sprinkle with remaining ½ cup cheese. Bake 1 to 3 minutes longer or until cheese is melted.

High Altitude (3500–6500 ft): No change.

1 SERVING: Calories 240 (Calories from Fat 80); Total Fat 8g (Saturated Fat 3g); Cholesterol 40mg; Sodium 770mg; Total Carbohydrate 20g (Dietary Fiber 1g); Protein 20g

Heart Smart Deluxe Turkey Cheeseburger Melt: Substitute 1 lb ground turkey breast for the extra-lean ground beef.

Cheesy Tomato-Beef Bake

PREP TIME: 15 MINUTES ▪ **START TO FINISH: 45 MINUTES**
10 SERVINGS

1 lb lean (at least 80%) ground beef

1 teaspoon chili powder

1 cup sour cream

²⁄₃ cup mayonnaise or salad dressing

1 cup shredded sharp Cheddar cheese (4 oz)

2 tablespoons finely chopped onion

2 cups Original Bisquick mix

½ cup cold water

2 to 3 medium tomatoes, thinly sliced

¾ cup chopped green bell pepper

1 Heat oven to 375°F. Spray 13 × 9-inch pan with cooking spray. In 10-inch skillet, cook beef and chili powder over medium-high heat 5 to 7 minutes, stirring frequently, until thoroughly cooked; drain.

2 In small bowl, stir sour cream, mayonnaise, cheese and onion until well mixed.

3 In medium bowl, stir Bisquick mix and cold water until soft dough forms. Press dough in bottom and ½ inch up sides of pan, using fingers dipped in Bisquick mix. Layer beef, tomatoes and bell pepper on dough. Spoon sour cream mixture over top; spread evenly over vegetables to cover.

4 Bake uncovered 25 to 30 minutes or until edges of dough are light golden brown.

High Altitude (3500-6500 ft): Bake uncovered 30 to 35 minutes.

1 SERVING: Calories 380 (Calories from Fat 250); Total Fat 28g (Saturated Fat 10g); Cholesterol 60mg; Sodium 480mg; Total Carbohydrate 19g (Dietary Fiber 1g); Protein 14g

Cheesy Tomato-Chicken Bake: Substitute 2 cups diced cooked chicken for the ground beef. Omit cooking beef and chili powder in step 1; toss the chicken with the chili powder and continue with step 2.

Beef and Potato Biscuit Casserole

PREP TIME: 15 MINUTES ▪ **START TO FINISH: 45 MINUTES**
6 SERVINGS

1 lb lean (at least 80%) ground beef

1 large onion, chopped (1 cup)

1 package (8 oz) sliced fresh mushrooms

1 teaspoon salt

$3/4$ cup water

2 tablespoons butter or margarine

1 cup plain mashed potato mix (dry)

$3/4$ cup sour cream

$2/3$ cup Original Bisquick mix

2 teaspoons chopped fresh chives

1 egg

1 can (18 oz) creamy mushroom soup

3 tablespoons Original Bisquick mix

1 bag (1 lb) frozen broccoli cuts, thawed, drained

$1/4$ cup ketchup

1 Heat oven to 400°F. In 12-inch skillet, cook beef, onion, mushrooms and salt over medium-high heat 5 to 7 minutes, stirring frequently, until beef is thoroughly cooked; drain.

2 While beef is cooking, in 2-quart saucepan, heat water and butter to boiling; remove from heat. Stir in potato mix and sour cream. Let stand 1 minute. Stir vigorously until smooth. Stir in $2/3$ cup Bisquick mix, the chives and egg.

3 In small bowl, mix soup and 3 tablespoons Bisquick mix. Stir soup mixture, broccoli and ketchup into beef mixture. Heat to boiling. Boil uncovered 1 minute. Pour mixture into ungreased 3-quart casserole. Spoon potato mixture around edge of mixture in casserole.

4 Bake uncovered 25 to 30 minutes or until biscuits are light golden brown.

High Altitude (3500–6500 ft): In step 1, cook over high heat. Bake 30 to 35 minutes.

1 SERVING: Calories 460 (Calories from Fat 240); Total Fat 26g (Saturated Fat 11g); Cholesterol 115mg; Sodium 1410mg; Total Carbohydrate 35g (Dietary Fiber 4g); Protein 22g

very Good

Cowboy Casserole

PREP TIME: 15 MINUTES ■ **START TO FINISH: 45 MINUTES**
6 SERVINGS

1 lb lean (at least 80%)
  ground beef

1 can (16 oz) baked beans

½ cup barbecue sauce

2 cups Original Bisquick mix

⅔ cup milk

1 tablespoon butter or
  margarine, softened

½ cup shredded Cheddar
  cheese (2 oz)

1 Heat oven to 425°F. In 10-inch skillet, cook beef over medium-high heat 5 to 7 minutes, stirring frequently, until thoroughly cooked; drain. Stir in baked beans and barbecue sauce. Heat to boiling, stirring occasionally. Pour into ungreased 2-quart casserole.

2 Meanwhile, in medium bowl, stir Bisquick mix, milk and butter until soft dough forms. Drop dough by 12 spoonfuls onto beef mixture.

3 Bake uncovered 18 to 22 minutes or until topping is golden brown. Sprinkle with cheese. Bake about 3 minutes longer or until cheese is melted.

High Altitude (3500-6500 ft): No change.

1 SERVING: Calories 470 (Calories from Fat 180); Total Fat 20g (Saturated Fat 8g); Cholesterol 70mg; Sodium 1160mg; Total Carbohydrate 50g (Dietary Fiber 5g); Protein 23g

Slow Cooker Burgundy Stew with Herb Dumplings

PREP TIME: 25 MINUTES ■ **START TO FINISH: 11 HOURS**
8 SERVINGS

STEW

2 lb boneless beef bottom or top round, tip or chuck steak, cut into 1-inch pieces

4 medium carrots, cut into 1/4-inch slices (2 cups)

2 medium stalks celery, sliced (1 cup)

2 medium onions, sliced

1 can (14.5 oz) diced tomatoes, undrained

1 can (8 oz) sliced mushrooms, drained

3/4 cup dry red wine or beef broth

1 1/2 teaspoons salt

1 teaspoon dried thyme leaves

1 teaspoon ground mustard

1/4 teaspoon pepper

1/4 cup water

3 tablespoons all-purpose flour

HERB DUMPLINGS

1 1/2 cups Original Bisquick mix

1/2 teaspoon dried thyme leaves

1/4 teaspoon dried sage leaves, crumbled

1/2 cup milk

1 In 4- to 6-quart slow cooker, mix all stew ingredients except water and flour.

2 Cover; cook on Low heat setting 8 to 10 hours (or High heat setting 4 to 5 hours).

3 In small bowl, stir water and flour until well mixed; gradually stir into beef mixture.

4 For dumplings, in medium bowl, stir Bisquick mix, thyme, sage and milk just until moistened. Drop dough by spoonfuls onto hot beef mixture. Increase heat setting to High. Cover; cook 25 to 35 minutes or until toothpick inserted in center of dumplings comes out clean.

High Altitude (3500–6500 ft): In step 2, for Low heat setting, cook 10 to 12 hours. For High heat setting, cook 5 to 6 hours.

1 SERVING: Calories 300 (Calories from Fat 60); Total Fat 7g (Saturated Fat 2.5g); Cholesterol 65mg; Sodium 970mg; Total Carbohydrate 27g (Dietary Fiber 3g); Protein 30g

Beef Pot Pie with Potato Crust

PREP TIME: 20 MINUTES ▪ **START TO FINISH: 55 MINUTES**
6 SERVINGS

1 slice (½ lb) deli roast beef, cubed (1½ cups)

2 cups frozen mixed vegetables

1 medium onion, chopped (½ cup)

1 jar (12 oz) beef gravy

⅔ cup plain mashed potato mix (dry)

⅔ cup hot water

1½ cups Original Bisquick mix

3 tablespoons milk

1 tablespoon freeze-dried chopped chives

1 Heat oven to 375°F. In 2-quart saucepan, heat beef, frozen vegetables, onion and gravy to boiling over medium heat, stirring frequently. Boil and stir 1 minute. Keep warm.

2 In medium bowl, stir potato mix and hot water until well mixed; let stand until water is absorbed. Stir in Bisquick mix, milk and chives until dough forms.

3 Place dough on surface sprinkled with Bisquick mix; gently roll in Bisquick mix to coat. Shape into a ball; knead 10 times. Press into 11 × 7-inch rectangle. Fold dough crosswise into thirds.

4 Pour beef mixture into ungreased 11 × 7-inch (2-quart) glass baking dish. Carefully unfold dough onto beef mixture.

5 Bake uncovered 30 to 35 minutes or until crust is golden brown.

High Altitude (3500-6500 ft): Bake uncovered 35 to 40 minutes.

1 SERVING: Calories 260 (Calories from Fat 60); Total Fat 6g (Saturated Fat 2.5g); Cholesterol 20mg; Sodium 1100mg; Total Carbohydrate 37g (Dietary Fiber 4g); Protein 14g

Chicken Pot Pie with Potato Crust: Substitute 1½ cups cooked cubed chicken for the beef and chicken gravy for beef gravy.

Roast Beef and Swiss Sandwich Bake

PREP TIME: 10 MINUTES ■ **START TO FINISH: 1 HOUR 5 MINUTES**
6 SERVINGS

2 cups Original Bisquick mix

1 cup milk

2 tablespoons yellow mustard

1 egg

1 package (6 oz) thinly sliced
  cooked roast beef, chopped

1 cup shredded Swiss cheese
  (4 oz)

Freshly ground pepper,
  if desired

1 Heat oven to 350°F. Grease 8-inch square glass baking dish.

2 In medium bowl, stir Bisquick mix, milk, mustard and egg until blended. Pour half of the batter into baking dish. Top with half of the roast beef and ½ cup of the cheese. Top with remaining roast beef. Pour remaining batter over roast beef.

3 Bake uncovered 45 to 50 minutes or until deep golden brown and center is set. Sprinkle with remaining ½ cup cheese and the pepper. Let stand 5 minutes before serving.

High Altitude (3500–6500 ft): Sprinkle with cheese to within ¼ inch of edges of baking dish. Bake 47 to 52 minutes.

1 SERVING: Calories 330 (Calories from Fat 155); Total Fat 17g (Saturated Fat 7g); 75mg; Sodium 730mg; Total Carbohydrate 27g (Dietary Fiber 1g); Protein 18g

Chili with Cornbread Dumplings

PREP TIME: 15 MINUTES ▪ **START TO FINISH: 55 MINUTES**
6 SERVINGS

1½ lb ground beef

1 large onion, chopped (¾ cup)

1 can (15.25 oz) whole kernel corn, undrained

1 can (14.5 oz) stewed tomatoes, undrained

1 can (16 oz) tomato sauce

2 tablespoons chili powder

1 teaspoon red pepper sauce

1⅓ cups Original Bisquick mix

⅔ cup cornmeal

⅔ cup milk

3 tablespoons chopped fresh cilantro or parsley, if desired

1 In 4-quart Dutch oven, cook beef and onion over medium heat, stirring occasionally, until beef is brown; drain. Reserve ½ cup of the corn. Stir remaining corn with liquid, tomatoes, tomato sauce, chili powder and pepper sauce into beef mixture. Heat to boiling; reduce heat. Cover and simmer 15 minutes.

2 In medium bowl, mix Bisquick mix and cornmeal. Stir in milk, cilantro and reserved ½ cup corn just until moistened.

3 Heat chili to boiling. Drop dough by rounded tablespoonfuls onto chili; reduce heat to low. Cook uncovered 10 minutes. Cover and cook about 10 minutes longer or until dumplings are dry.

High Altitude (3500–6500 ft): After dropping dough onto chili, cook uncovered over low heat 15 minutes. Cover and cook 15 to 18 minutes longer or until dumplings are dry.

1 SERVING: Calories 515 (Calories from Fat 200); Total Fat 22g (Saturated Fat 8g); Cholesterol 65mg; Sodium 1310mg; Total Carbohydrate 56g (Dietary Fiber 6g); Protein 29g

Sausage Chili Bake

PREP TIME: 15 MINUTES ▪ **START TO FINISH: 55 MINUTES**
10 SERVINGS

1 lb smoked sausage, cut into ½-inch slices

1 small onion, chopped (½ cup)

1 teaspoon garlic salt

1 to 2 tablespoons chili powder

1 can (14.5 oz) stewed tomatoes, undrained

1 can (15 to 16 oz) kidney beans, undrained

2 cups Original Bisquick mix

½ cup cornmeal

1 cup milk

2 eggs

1 Heat oven to 350°F. Spray 10-inch skillet with cooking spray; heat over medium-high heat. In skillet, cook sausage and onion 4 to 5 minutes, stirring occasionally, until onion is tender.

2 Spoon mixture into ungreased 13 × 9-inch (3-quart) glass baking dish. Stir in garlic salt, chili powder, tomatoes and beans. In medium bowl, stir remaining ingredients with wire whisk or fork until blended. Pour over sausage mixture.

3 Bake uncovered 35 to 40 minutes or until crust is light golden brown.

High Altitude (3500–6500 ft): No change.

1 SERVING: Calories 350 (Calories from Fat 160); Total Fat 18g (Saturated Fat 6g); Cholesterol 70mg; Sodium 1050mg; Total Carbohydrate 36g (Dietary Fiber 4g); Protein 13g

Fall Pork Dinner

PREP TIME: 20 MINUTES ■ **START TO FINISH: 1 HOUR 5 MINUTES**
3 SERVINGS

¼ cup packed brown sugar

½ teaspoon ground cinnamon

1 tablespoon firm butter or margarine, cut up

½ small acorn squash

1 small unpeeled red cooking apple

⅓ cup Bisquick Heart Smart mix

½ teaspoon seasoned salt

⅛ teaspoon pepper

5 saltine crackers, crushed

1 egg white or 2 tablespoons fat-free egg product

1 tablespoon water

3 boneless pork loin chops, ½ inch thick (¾ lb)

1 Heat oven to 350°F. In small bowl, mix brown sugar, cinnamon and butter until crumbly; set aside. Cut squash into ½-inch rings; remove seeds. Cut apple into chunks.

2 In shallow dish, stir Bisquick mix, seasoned salt, pepper and cracker crumbs. In another shallow dish, mix egg white and water. Dip pork into egg mixture, then coat with Bisquick mixture.

3 Spray 10-inch skillet with cooking spray; heat over medium-high heat. In skillet, cook pork 6 to 8 minutes, turning once, until coating is brown. Place pork in ungreased 8-inch square or 11 × 7-inch (2-quart) glass baking dish. Arrange squash and apples around pork. Sprinkle with brown sugar mixture.

4 Bake uncovered 40 to 45 minutes or until squash is tender and pork is no longer pink in center.

High Altitude (3500-6500 ft): No change.

1 SERVING: Calories 410 (Calories from Fat 130); Total Fat 14g (Saturated Fat 6g); Cholesterol 80mg; Sodium 530mg; Total Carbohydrate 43g (Dietary Fiber 3g); Protein 28g

Oven-Fried Pork Cutlets with Apple Slaw

PREP TIME: 10 MINUTES ■ **START TO FINISH: 30 MINUTES**
4 SERVINGS

PORK CUTLETS

4 boneless pork loin chops, ½ inch thick (about 1 lb)

8 saltine crackers, finely crushed (⅓ cup)

½ cup Original Bisquick mix

½ teaspoon paprika

¼ teaspoon pepper

1 egg or ¼ cup fat-free egg product

1 tablespoon water

Cooking spray

APPLE SLAW

4 cups coleslaw mix (shredded cabbage and carrots)

1 small tart red apple, coarsely chopped (1 cup)

¼ cup chopped onion

⅓ cup fat-free coleslaw dressing

⅛ teaspoon celery seed

1 Heat oven to 425°F. Generously spray 15 × 10 × 1-inch pan with cooking spray. Between pieces of plastic wrap or waxed paper, place each pork chop; gently pound with flat side of meat mallet or rolling pin until about ¼ inch thick.

2 In small shallow dish, mix crackers, Bisquick mix, paprika and pepper. In another shallow dish, beat egg and water. Dip pork chops into egg, then coat with cracker mixture. Repeat dipping coated pork in egg and in cracker mixture. Place in pan. Generously spray tops of pork with cooking spray.

3 Bake about 20 minutes or until pork chops are golden brown and no longer pink in center.

4 Meanwhile, in large bowl, toss all apple slaw ingredients. Serve slaw with pork cutlets.

High Altitude (3500–6500 ft): No change.

1 SERVING: Calories 360 (Calories from Fat 130); Total Fat 14g (Saturated Fat 4.5g); Cholesterol 125mg; Sodium 480mg; Total Carbohydrate 29g (Dietary Fiber 3g); Protein 29g

Impossibly Easy Ham and Swiss Pie

PREP TIME: 10 MINUTES ▪ **START TO FINISH: 55 MINUTES**

6 SERVINGS

1½ cups cut-up fully cooked ham

1 cup shredded Swiss cheese (4 oz)

4 medium green onions, sliced (¼ cup)

½ cup Original Bisquick mix

1 cup milk

¼ teaspoon salt

⅛ teaspoon pepper

2 eggs

1 Heat oven to 400°F. Grease 9-inch pie plate. In pie plate, sprinkle ham, cheese and onions.

2 In medium bowl, stir remaining ingredients with fork until blended. Pour into pie plate.

3 Bake 35 to 40 minutes or until knife inserted in center comes out clean. Let stand 5 minutes before serving.

High Altitude (3500-6500 ft): Bake about 45 minutes.

1 SERVING: Calories 215 (Calories from Fat 110); Total Fat 12g (Saturated Fat 6g); Cholesterol 110mg; Sodium 830mg; Total Carbohydrate 10g (Dietary Fiber 0g); Protein 17g

Easy Salmon Puff

PREP TIME: 15 MINUTES ■ **START TO FINISH: 55 MINUTES**
6 SERVINGS

1 cup Original Bisquick mix

1 teaspoon dried dill weed

1 cup milk

½ cup sour cream

4 eggs

2 cans (6 oz each) boneless skinless salmon, drained, flaked

1 cup shredded Havarti or Swiss cheese (4 oz)

1 Heat oven to 375°F. Spray 9-inch glass pie plate with cooking spray. In medium bowl, stir Bisquick mix, dill weed, milk, sour cream and eggs with wire whisk or fork until blended. Gently stir in salmon and cheese. Pour into pie plate.

2 Bake uncovered 35 to 40 minutes or until knife inserted in center comes out clean.

High Altitude (3500–6500 ft): Bake uncovered 38 to 43 minutes.

1 SERVING: Calories 350 (Calories from Fat 180); Total Fat 20g (Saturated Fat 10g); Cholesterol 225mg; Sodium 680mg; Total Carbohydrate 17g (Dietary Fiber 1g); Protein 25g

Easy Tuna Puff: Substitute 2 cans (6 ounces each) tuna, drained, for the salmon.

CHAPTER 5

Delicious
Desserts

Velvet Crumb Cake

PREP TIME: 15 MINUTES ▪ START TO FINISH: 1 HOUR 10 MINUTES
8 SERVINGS

CAKE

1½ cups Original Bisquick mix

½ cup sugar

½ cup milk or water

2 tablespoons shortening

1 teaspoon vanilla

1 egg

TOPPING

½ cup flaked coconut

⅓ cup packed brown sugar

¼ cup chopped nuts

3 tablespoons butter or
   margarine, softened

2 tablespoons milk

1 Heat oven to 350°F. Grease and flour 8-inch square pan or 9-inch round cake pan, or spray with baking spray with flour. In large bowl, beat all cake ingredients with electric mixer on low speed 30 seconds, scraping bowl constantly. Beat on medium speed 4 minutes, scraping bowl occasionally. Pour into pan.

2 Bake 30 to 35 minutes or until toothpick inserted in center comes out clean. Cool slightly, about 15 minutes.

3 Set oven control to broil. In small bowl, mix all topping ingredients until crumbly. Spread topping over cake. Broil cake with top 3 inches from heat about 3 minutes or until topping is golden brown.

High Altitude (3500–6500 ft): Heat oven to 375°F. Decrease Bisquick mix to 1⅓ cups and add ⅓ cup all-purpose flour. Increase milk to ⅔ cup. Bake about 25 minutes.

1 SERVING: Calories 310 (Calories from Fat 140); Total Fat 15g (Saturated Fat 7g); Cholesterol 40mg; Sodium 340mg; Total Carbohydrate 40g (Dietary Fiber 1g); Protein 4g

Honey-Apple Cake

PREP TIME: 20 MINUTES ▪ START TO FINISH: 2 HOURS 25 MINUTES
12 SERVINGS

CAKE

1 cup chopped pecans

3½ cups Original Bisquick mix

1 teaspoon ground cinnamon

¼ teaspoon ground nutmeg

1½ cups granulated sugar

½ cup vegetable oil

¼ cup honey

3 eggs

1 teaspoon vanilla

3 cups chopped medium tart
 cooking apples (Haralson
 or Granny Smith)

SAUCE AND TOPPING

1 cup packed brown sugar

½ cup butter or margarine

¼ cup honey

¼ cup milk

Vanilla ice cream

1 Heat oven to 350°F. Grease and flour 12-cup fluted tube cake pan. Sprinkle bottom of pan with ¼ cup of the pecans; set aside. In medium bowl, stir Bisquick mix, cinnamon and nutmeg; set aside.

2 In large bowl, beat granulated sugar, oil and ¼ cup honey with electric mixer on medium speed 30 seconds. Add eggs, one at a time, beating well after each addition. Gradually add Bisquick mixture to sugar mixture, beating at low speed just until blended. Stir in vanilla, remaining ¾ cups pecans and the apples. Spoon over pecans in pan.

3 Bake 55 to 60 minutes or until toothpick inserted in center comes out clean. Cool in pan on cooling rack 15 minutes.

4 In 2-quart saucepan, heat brown sugar, butter, ¼ cup honey and the milk to boiling over medium-high heat, stirring constantly. Boil, stirring constantly, 2 minutes. Remove cake from pan to cooling rack. Pour ½ cup sauce over warm cake. Cool completely, about 1 hour. Serve remaining sauce with cake. Top with ice cream, if desired.

High Altitude (3500–6500 ft): Bake 1 hour to 1 hour 5 minutes.

1 SERVING: Calories 690 (Calories from Fat 300); Total Fat 33g (Saturated Fat 11g); Cholesterol 90mg; Sodium 540mg; Total Carbohydrate 92g (Dietary Fiber 3g); Protein 7g

Caramel-Apple Cake

PREP TIME: 20 MINUTES ▪ **START TO FINISH: 1 HOUR 20 MINUTES**
6 SERVINGS

1½ cups Original Bisquick mix

⅔ cup granulated sugar

½ cup milk

2 medium cooking apples, peeled and sliced (2 cups)

1 tablespoon lemon juice

¾ cup packed brown sugar

½ teaspoon ground cinnamon

1 cup boiling water

Ice cream or whipped cream, if desired

1 Heat oven to 350°F. In medium bowl, mix Bisquick mix and granulated sugar. Stir in milk until blended.

2 Pour batter into ungreased 9-inch square pan. Top with apples; sprinkle with lemon juice. Mix brown sugar and cinnamon; sprinkle over apples. Pour boiling water over apples.

3 Bake 50 to 60 minutes or until toothpick inserted in center comes out clean. Serve warm with ice cream.

High Altitude (over 3500 ft): Not recommended.

1 SERVING: Calories 355 (Calories from Fat 45); Total Fat 5g (Saturated Fat 1g); Cholesterol 0mg; Sodium 450mg; Total Carbohydrate 75g (Dietary Fiber 1g); Protein 3g

Cream Cheese Pound Cake

PREP TIME: 15 MINUTES ■ START TO FINISH: 2 HOURS 20 MINUTES

10 SERVINGS

3 cups Original Bisquick mix

1½ cups granulated sugar

¾ cup butter or margarine, softened

½ cup all-purpose flour

1 teaspoon vanilla

⅛ teaspoon salt

6 eggs

1 package (8 oz) cream cheese, softened

Powdered sugar, if desired

1 Heat oven to 350°F. Grease and flour 12-cup fluted tube cake pan or two 9-inch loaf pans.

2 In large bowl, beat all ingredients except powdered sugar with electric mixer on low speed 30 seconds, scraping bowl frequently. Beat on medium speed 4 minutes, scraping bowl occasionally. Pour into pan.

3 Bake 55 to 60 minutes or until toothpick inserted near center comes out clean. Cool 5 minutes. Turn pan upside down on cooling rack or heatproof serving plate; remove pan. Cool cake completely, about 1 hour. Sprinkle with powdered sugar.

High Altitude (3500–6500 ft): Heat oven to 375°F. Do not use loaf pans. Use 2½ cups Bisquick mix, 1¼ cups granulated sugar and 1 cup flour. Bake 45 to 50 minutes.

1 SERVING: Calories 535 (Calories from Fat 270); Total Fat 30g (Saturated Fat 10g); Cholesterol 150mg; Sodium 830mg; Total Carbohydrate 58g (Dietary Fiber 1g); Protein 9g

ocolate-Cinnamon Sundae Cake

PREP TIME: 20 MINUTES ■ **START TO FINISH: 55 MINUTES**
9 SERVINGS

CHOCOLATE-CINNAMON SAUCE

1 cup chocolate-flavored syrup

½ teaspoon ground cinnamon

CAKE

1⅓ cups Bisquick Heart Smart mix

½ cup sugar

⅓ cup baking cocoa

1 teaspoon ground cinnamon

¼ cup fat-free cholesterol-free egg product, 2 egg whites or 1 egg

⅔ cup fat-free (skim) milk

3 tablespoons butter or margarine, softened

1 pint (2 cups) reduced-fat vanilla ice cream, if desired

1 Heat oven to 350°F. Grease and flour 8-inch square pan.

2 In medium bowl, beat all cake ingredients except ice cream and sauce ingredients with electric mixer on low speed 30 seconds, scraping bowl frequently. Beat on medium speed 4 minutes, scraping bowl occasionally. Pour into pan.

3 Bake 30 to 35 minutes or until toothpick inserted in center comes out clean.

4 Meanwhile, in 1-quart saucepan, heat all sauce ingredients over medium-low heat, stirring occasionally, until warm. Serve sauce warm or cool. Drizzle sauce over warm or cool cake. Serve with ice cream.

High Altitude (3500–6500 ft): No change.

1 SERVING: Calories 240 (Calories from Fat 55); Total Fat 6g (Saturated Fat 1g); Cholesterol 0mg; Sodium 300mg; Total Carbohydrate 45g (Dietary Fiber 2g); Protein 4g

Cherry-Pecan Ring

PREP TIME: 15 MINUTES ▪ **START TO FINISH: 50 MINUTES**
10 SERVINGS

COFFEE CAKE

⅓ cup butter or margarine, melted

⅓ cup packed brown sugar

1 jar (6 oz) maraschino cherries (about 25 cherries), drained, stems removed

⅓ cup pecan halves

2 cups Original Bisquick mix

2 tablespoons granulated sugar

⅔ cup milk

2 tablespoons butter or margarine, softened

1 egg

GLAZE

1 cup powdered sugar

4 teaspoons water

½ teaspoon vanilla

1 Heat oven to 400°F. Spray 8-cup fluted tube cake pan with cooking spray. Pour ⅓ cup melted butter into pan; turn pan to coat with butter. Sprinkle brown sugar over butter. Arrange cherries and pecans on sugar mixture.

2 In medium bowl, stir Bisquick mix, granulated sugar, milk, 2 tablespoons softened butter and egg until combined; beat vigorously 30 seconds. Spoon batter evenly over cherries and pecans.

3 Bake 20 to 25 minutes or until toothpick inserted in center comes out clean. Immediately place heatproof plate upside down on pan; carefully turn plate and pan over to remove coffee cake. Cool 10 minutes.

4 In small bowl, mix all glaze ingredients until smooth and thin enough to drizzle, adding additional water, 1 teaspoon at a time, to desired consistency. Drizzle glaze over warm coffee cake.

High Altitude (3500-6500 ft): No change.

1 SERVING: Calories 320 (Calories from Fat 130); Total Fat 15g (Saturated Fat 7g); Cholesterol 45mg; Sodium 370mg; Total Carbohydrate 43g (Dietary Fiber 1g); Protein 3g

Classic Strawberry Shortcakes

PREP TIME: 10 MINUTES ▪ START TO FINISH: 1 HOUR 40 MINUTES
6 SERVINGS

1 quart (4 cups) fresh
    strawberries, sliced

½ cup sugar

2⅓ cups Original Bisquick mix

3 tablespoons sugar

½ cup milk

3 tablespoons butter or
    margarine, melted

¾ cup whipped cream or frozen
    (thawed) whipped topping

1 In medium bowl, toss strawberries and ½ cup sugar until coated. Let stand 1 hour.

2 Heat oven to 425°F. In medium bowl, stir Bisquick mix, 3 tablespoons sugar, the milk and butter until soft dough forms. On ungreased cookie sheet, drop dough by 6 spoonfuls.

3 Bake 10 to 12 minutes or until golden brown. Cool 15 minutes. Using knife, split warm shortcakes. Fill and top with strawberries and whipped cream.

High Altitude (3500–6500 ft): Heat oven to 450°F. Decrease sugar in shortcakes to 1 tablespoon.

1 SERVING: Calories 400 (Calories from Fat 130); Total Fat 14g (Saturated Fat 7g); Cholesterol 15mg; Sodium 620mg; Total Carbohydrate 64g (Dietary Fiber 3g); Protein 5g

Mango-Lime Shortcakes

PREP TIME: 10 MINUTES ■ **START TO FINISH: 35 MINUTES**
2 SERVINGS

⅔ cup Bisquick Heart Smart mix

1 tablespoon sugar

1 teaspoon grated lime peel

2 tablespoons fat-free (skim) milk

2 teaspoons vegetable oil

1 snack-size container (4 oz) refrigerated vanilla pudding snack (from 6-snack package)

1 tablespoon lime juice

½ teaspoon grated lime peel

½ cup refrigerated mango in light syrup (from 1-lb 8-oz-jar), drained, cubed

Whipped topping, if desired

1 Heat oven to 375°F. Spray cookie sheet with cooking spray. In medium bowl, stir Bisquick mix, sugar, 1 teaspoon lime peel, the milk and oil until soft dough forms. Drop dough by 2 spoonfuls on cookie sheet.

2 Bake 9 to 12 minutes or until golden brown. Cool 10 minutes.

3 Meanwhile, in small bowl, mix pudding, lime juice and ½ teaspoon lime peel until well blended.

4 Split warm shortcakes. Fill and top with mango and pudding mixture. Top with whipped topping.

High Altitude (3500–6500 ft): Add up to 2 teaspoons more milk if necessary to make a soft dough. Bake 12 to 15 minutes.

1 SERVING: Calories 330 (Calories from Fat 80); Total Fat 9g (Saturated Fat 1.5g); Cholesterol 0mg; Sodium 520mg; Total Carbohydrate 57g (Dietary Fiber 0g); Protein 5g

Meringue-Topped Strawberry Shortcake

PREP TIME: 25 MINUTES ■ START TO FINISH: 2 HOURS 50 MINUTES
8 SERVINGS

1 quart (4 cups) fresh
   strawberries, sliced

1/4 cup granulated sugar

2 1/3 cups Original Bisquick mix

3 tablespoons granulated sugar

3 tablespoons butter or
   margarine, melted

1/2 cup milk

2 egg whites

1/4 cup powdered sugar

1/4 cup granulated sugar

1 tablespoon granulated sugar

1 In medium bowl, toss strawberries with 1/4 cup granulated sugar. Let stand 1 hour.

2 Meanwhile, heat oven to 375°F. In medium bowl, stir Bisquick mix, 3 tablespoons granulated sugar, the butter and milk until soft dough forms. Place on surface sprinkled with Bisquick mix. Shape into a ball; knead 8 to 10 times. Press dough in ungreased 9-inch round cake pan.

3 In medium bowl, beat egg whites until foamy. Beat in powdered sugar and 1/4 cup granulated sugar, 1 tablespoon at a time; beating until stiff and glossy. Spread meringue on dough; sprinkle with 1 tablespoon granulated sugar.

4 Bake about 30 minutes or until golden brown. Cool 10 minutes. Run knife around edge of pan to loosen shortcake; turn onto cloth-covered cooling rack or plate. Turn meringue side up onto rack. Cool completely, about 1 hour. Serve with strawberries.

High Altitude (over 3500 ft): No change.

1 SERVING: Calories 310 (Calories from Fat 80); Total Fat 9g (Saturated Fat 4.5g); Cholesterol 15mg; Sodium 480mg; Total Carbohydrate 52g (Dietary Fiber 2g); Protein 5g

ssibly Easy Toffee Bar Cheesecake

PREP TIME: 10 MINUTES ▪ **START TO FINISH: 5 HOURS 45 MINUTES**
8 SERVINGS

¼ cup milk

2 teaspoons vanilla

2 eggs

¾ cup packed brown sugar

¼ cup Original Bisquick mix

2 packages (8 oz each) cream cheese, cut into 16 pieces, softened

3 bars (1.4 oz each) chocolate-covered English toffee candy, coarsely chopped

½ cup caramel topping

1 Heat oven to 325°F. Spray bottom of 9-inch glass pie plate with cooking spray.

2 In blender, place milk, vanilla, eggs, brown sugar and Bisquick mix. Cover; blend on high speed 15 seconds. Add cream cheese. Cover; blend 2 minutes. Pour into pie plate.

3 Sprinkle candy over top; swirl gently with table knife to evenly distribute candy.

4 Bake 30 to 35 minutes or until about 2 inches of edge of pie is set and center is still soft and wiggles slightly. Cool completely, about 1 hour.

5 Refrigerate at least 4 hours. Serve with caramel topping. Store in refrigerator.

High Altitude (3500–6500 ft): No change.

1 SERVING: Calories 460 (Calories from Fat 240); Total Fat 27g (Saturated Fat 16g); Cholesterol 125mg; Sodium 360mg; Total Carbohydrate 47g (Dietary Fiber 0g); Protein 7g

Impossibly Easy Mocha Fudge Cheesecake

PREP TIME: 10 MINUTES ▪ **START TO FINISH: 3 HOURS 50 MINUTES**
8 SERVINGS

CHEESECAKE

1 tablespoon instant coffee granules or crystals

3 tablespoons coffee liqueur or strong brewed coffee, cooled to room temperature

2 packages (8 oz each) cream cheese, softened

¾ cup Original Bisquick mix

¾ cup sugar

1 teaspoon vanilla

3 eggs

3 oz semisweet baking chocolate, melted and cooled

CHOCOLATE TOPPING

1 oz semisweet baking chocolate, melted and cooled

2 tablespoons powdered sugar

1 tablespoon coffee liqueur, if desired

1 container (8 oz) sour cream

1 teaspoon vanilla

1 Heat oven to 350°F. Grease 9-inch pie plate. In small bowl, stir coffee and liqueur until coffee is dissolved.

2 In large bowl, beat coffee mixture and remaining cheesecake ingredients with electric mixer on high speed about 2 minutes, scraping bowl frequently, until well blended. Pour into pie plate.

3 Bake about 35 minutes or until center is firm and puffed. Cool 5 minutes (top of cheesecake will be cracked).

4 For topping, in small bowl, stir chocolate, powdered sugar and liqueur until blended. Stir in sour cream and vanilla. Carefully spread topping over cheesecake. Refrigerate at least 3 hours before serving. Store covered in refrigerator.

High Altitude (3500–6500 ft): Bake about 40 minutes.

1 SERVING: Calories 490 (Calories from Fat 295); Total Fat 33g (Saturated Fat 19g); Cholesterol 160mg; Sodium 360mg; Total Carbohydrate 40g (Dietary Fiber 1g); Protein 9g

Impossibly Easy French Apple Pie

PREP TIME: 25 MINUTES ● **START TO FINISH: 1 HOUR 15 MINUTES**
8 SERVINGS

STREUSEL TOPPING

½ cup Original Bisquick mix

¼ cup chopped nuts

¼ cup packed brown sugar

2 tablespoons firm butter or margarine

APPLE PIE

3 large all-purpose apples (Braeburn, Gala or Haralson), peeled and thinly sliced (3 cups)

½ cup Original Bisquick mix

½ cup sugar

½ cup milk

1 tablespoon butter or margarine, softened

1 teaspoon ground cinnamon

¼ teaspoon ground nutmeg

2 eggs

1 Heat oven to 350°F. Grease 9-inch glass pie plate. In medium bowl, mix apples, cinnamon and nutmeg; place in pie plate.

2 In medium bowl, stir remaining pie ingredients until well blended. Pour over apple mixture in pie plate. In small bowl, mix all streusel ingredients until crumbly; sprinkle over filling.

3 Bake 40 to 45 minutes or until knife inserted in center comes out clean. Cool 5 minutes. Store in refrigerator.

High Altitude (3500-6500 ft): Heat oven to 375°F.

1 SERVING: Calories 235 (Calories from Fat 90); Total Fat 10g (Saturated Fat 2g); Cholesterol 55mg; Sodium 290mg; Total Carbohydrate 33g (Dietary Fiber 1g); Protein 4g

Impossibly Easy Banana Custard Pie

PREP TIME: 15 MINUTES ■ **START TO FINISH: 4 HOURS**

8 SERVINGS

1 cup mashed ripe bananas (2 medium)

2 teaspoons lemon juice

½ cup Original Bisquick mix

¼ cup sugar

1 tablespoon butter or margarine, softened

½ teaspoon vanilla

2 eggs

1 can (14 oz) sweetened condensed milk

¾ cup frozen (thawed) whipped topping

¼ cup coarsely chopped walnuts, if desired

Caramel topping, warmed, if desired

1 Heat oven to 350°F. Grease 9-inch glass pie plate. In small bowl, mix bananas and lemon juice; set aside.

2 In medium bowl, stir Bisquick mix, sugar, butter, vanilla, eggs and milk until blended. Add banana mixture; stir until blended. Pour into pie plate.

3 Bake 40 to 45 minutes or until golden brown and knife inserted in center comes out clean. Cool completely, about 1 hour. Cover and refrigerate about 2 hours or until chilled.

4 Spread pie with whipped topping; sprinkle with walnuts. Drizzle with caramel topping. Store covered in refrigerator.

High Altitude (3500-6500 ft): No change.

1 SERVING: Calories 345 (Calories from Fat 100); Total Fat 11g (Saturated Fat 5g); Cholesterol 75mg; Sodium 230mg; Total Carbohydrate 55g (Dietary Fiber 1g); Protein 8g

Impossibly Easy Pear-Custard Pie

PREP TIME: 15 MINUTES ▪ **START TO FINISH: 1 HOUR 25 MINUTES**
8 SERVINGS

STREUSEL

½ cup Original Bisquick mix

¼ cup quick-cooking or old-fashioned oats

¼ cup packed brown sugar

½ teaspoon ground nutmeg

1 tablespoon butter or margarine, softened

PIE

½ cup Original Bisquick mix

⅓ cup granulated sugar

½ cup milk

2 tablespoons butter or margarine, softened

2 eggs

3 medium fresh pears, peeled, sliced (about 3 cups)

1 Heat oven to 350°F. Spray 9-inch glass pie plate with cooking spray. In small bowl, stir ½ cup Bisquick mix, the oats, brown sugar and nutmeg. Cut in 1 tablespoon butter, using pastry blender (or pulling 2 table knives through ingredients in opposite directions), until crumbly. Set aside.

2 In medium bowl, stir all pie ingredients except pears with wire whisk or fork until blended. Pour into pie plate. Arrange pears evenly over top.

3 Bake 25 minutes. Sprinkle streusel over top. Bake 12 to 15 minutes longer or until knife inserted in center comes out clean. Cool 30 minutes. Serve warm. Store in refrigerator.

High Altitude (3500–6500 ft): No change.

1 SERVING: Calories 240 (Calories from Fat 70); Total Fat 8g (Saturated Fat 4g); Cholesterol 65mg; Sodium 240mg; Total Carbohydrate 37g (Dietary Fiber 2g); Protein 4g

Fluffy Key Lime Pie

PREP TIME: 30 MINUTES ▪ **START TO FINISH: 2 HOURS 40 MINUTES**
8 SERVINGS

PAT-IN-THE-PAN PIE CRUST

1 cup Original Bisquick mix

¼ cup butter or margarine, softened

2 tablespoons boiling water

KEY LIME PIE

1 can (14 oz) sweetened condensed milk

½ cup Key lime juice or regular lime juice

1 container (8 oz) frozen whipped topping, thawed

1 tablespoon grated lime peel

Lime slices, if desired

1 Heat oven to 400°F. For pie crust, in medium bowl, mix Bisquick mix and butter. Add boiling water; stir vigorously until very soft dough forms. Press dough firmly in 9-inch pie plate, bringing dough onto rim of plate, using fingers dusted with Bisquick mix. Flute edge if desired. Freeze 15 minutes. Bake 8 to 10 minutes or until light golden brown. Cool completely on cooling rack, about 30 minutes.

2 In large bowl, beat milk and lime juice with electric mixer on medium speed until smooth and thickened. Fold in whipped topping and lime peel. Spoon into pie crust.

3 Cover and refrigerate about 2 hours or until set. Garnish with lime slices. Store covered in refrigerator.

High Altitude (3500–6500 ft): Bake crust 10 to 12 minutes.

1 SERVING: Calories 355 (Calories from Fat 135); Total Fat 15g (Saturated Fat 8g); Cholesterol 40mg; Sodium 340mg; Total Carbohydrate 48g (Dietary Fiber 0g); Protein 7g

X

Quick Cherry Cobbler

PREP TIME: 10 MINUTES ▪ START TO FINISH: 30 MINUTES
6 SERVINGS

1 can (21 oz) cherry pie filling

1 cup Original Bisquick mix

1 tablespoon sugar

¼ cup milk

1 tablespoon butter or
    margarine, softened

Additional sugar, if desired

1 In ungreased 8-inch square pan, spread pie filling; place in cold oven. Heat oven to 400°F; heat 10 minutes. Remove pan from oven.

2 Meanwhile, stir Bisquick mix, 1 tablespoon sugar, the milk and butter until soft dough forms. On warm cherry mixture, drop dough by 6 spoonfuls. Sprinkle with additional sugar.

3 Bake 18 to 20 minutes or until topping is light golden brown.

High Altitude (3500–6500 ft): Heat oven to 425°F. Place pan with pie filling in HOT oven 15 minutes. Remove from oven. Drop dough by 6 spoonfuls. Bake 18 to 20 minutes.

1 SERVING: Calories 220 (Calories from Fat 45); Total Fat 5g (Saturated Fat 2g); Cholesterol 5mg; Sodium 260mg; Total Carbohydrate 42g (Dietary Fiber 2g); Protein 3g

Quick Peach Cobbler: Substitute 1 can (21 oz) peach pie filling for the cherry pie filling.

Lemon Biscuit Pudding

PREP TIME: 15 MINUTES ▪ **START TO FINISH: 40 MINUTES**
6 SERVINGS

BISCUITS

¼ cup sugar

2½ cups Original Bisquick mix

½ cup milk

1 teaspoon grated lemon peel

PUDDING

1 cup half-and-half

½ cup sugar

1 tablespoon grated lemon peel

1 egg

1 Heat oven to 450°F. Spray 8-inch square (2-quart) glass baking dish with cooking spray.

2 Reserve 1½ teaspoons of the ¼ cup sugar. In medium bowl, stir remaining sugar and remaining biscuit ingredients until soft dough forms. Drop dough by 9 spoonfuls into dish. Sprinkle reserved 1½ teaspoons sugar over top.

3 Bake 8 to 10 minutes or until light golden brown.

4 Meanwhile, in medium bowl, beat all pudding ingredients with wire whisk or fork until well blended. Pour over hot biscuits.

5 Reduce oven temperature to 350°F. Bake 18 to 20 minutes longer or until pudding is set and knife inserted in center comes out clean. Serve warm.

High Altitude (3500–6500 ft): In step 3, bake 12 to 14 minutes. In step 5, bake 20 to 22 minutes longer.

1 SERVING: Calories 380 (Calories from Fat 110); Total Fat 12g (Saturated Fat 5g); Cholesterol 50mg; Sodium 650mg; Total Carbohydrate 60g (Dietary Fiber 1g); Protein 7g

White Chocolate–Berry Bread Pudding

PREP TIME: 30 MINUTES ▪ **START TO FINISH: 10 HOURS 10 MINUTES**
12 SERVINGS

PUDDING

4½ cups Original Bisquick mix

1⅓ cups milk

¾ cup grated white chocolate baking bars

⅔ cup sugar

3½ cups milk

1½ cups whipping cream

2 tablespoons butter or margarine, melted

1 tablespoon vanilla

4 eggs

1 cup frozen unsweetened raspberries (do not thaw)

1 cup frozen unsweetened blueberries (do not thaw)

BERRY SAUCE

⅓ cup sugar

2 tablespoons Original Bisquick mix

1 cup frozen unsweetened raspberries (do not thaw)

1 cup frozen unsweetened blueberries (do not thaw)

½ cup water

Fresh berries, if desired

1 Heat oven to 450°F. Butter bottom and sides of 13 × 9-inch (3-quart) glass baking dish. In large bowl, stir 4½ cups Bisquick mix and 1⅓ cups milk until soft dough forms. On ungreased large cookie sheet, drop dough by heaping tablespoonfuls.

2 Bake 8 to 10 minutes or until golden. Cool on cooling rack, about 30 minutes.

3 Break up biscuits into random-sized pieces; spread in baking dish. Sprinkle with grated baking bars. In large bowl, beat ⅔ cup sugar, the milk, whipping cream, butter, vanilla and eggs with electric mixer on low speed until blended. Pour over biscuits in baking dish. Cover and refrigerate at least 8 hours but no longer than 24 hours.

4 Heat oven to 350°F. Stir 1 cup frozen raspberries and 1 cup frozen blueberries into biscuit mixture. Bake uncovered about 1 hour or until top is golden brown and toothpick inserted in center comes out clean.

5 In 1-quart saucepan, place ⅓ cup sugar and 2 tablespoons Bisquick mix. Stir in 1 cup frozen raspberries, 1 cup frozen blueberries and the water. Cook over medium heat, stirring constantly, until mixture thickens and boils. Boil and stir 1 minute; remove from heat. Serve pudding warm topped with sauce. Garnish with fresh berries. Store in refrigerator.

High Altitude (3500–6500 ft): Bake bread pudding about 1 hour 10 minutes.

1 SERVING: Calories 530 (Calories from Fat 210); Total Fat 24g (Saturated Fat 12g); Cholesterol 120mg; Sodium 660mg; Total Carbohydrate 67g (Dietary Fiber 5g); Protein 11g

Cinnamon-Apple Crisp

PREP TIME: 10 MINUTES ■ **START TO FINISH: 50 MINUTES**
12 SERVINGS

10 medium tart apples, peeled, thinly sliced (10 cups)

2 cups Original Bisquick mix

2 cups packed brown sugar

1 teaspoon ground cinnamon

½ cup firm butter or margarine

Ice cream, if desired

1 Heat oven to 375°F. In ungreased 13 × 9-inch pan, spread apples.

2 In medium bowl, stir Bisquick mix, brown sugar and cinnamon. Cut in butter using pastry blender (or pulling 2 table knives through ingredients in opposite directions), until mixture looks like fine crumbs. Sprinkle over apples.

3 Bake uncovered about 40 minutes or until apples are tender. Serve warm with ice cream.

High Altitude (3500–6500 ft): Heat oven to 400°F.

1 SERVING: Calories 340 (Calories from Fat 90); Total Fat 10g (Saturated Fat 6g); Cholesterol 20mg; Sodium 310mg; Total Carbohydrate 61g (Dietary Fiber 2g); Protein 2g

Raspberry Truffle Tart

PREP TIME: 30 MINUTES ▪ **START TO FINISH: 4 HOURS 5 MINUTES**
12 SERVINGS

1¼ cups Original Bisquick mix

½ cup powdered sugar

½ cup finely chopped pecans

¼ cup firm butter or margarine

1 tablespoon hot water

⅔ cup raspberry preserves, melted

1 cup whipping cream

1 bag (12 oz) semisweet chocolate chips (2 cups)

2 tablespoons raspberry liqueur, if desired

1 pint (2 cups) raspberries

1 Heat oven to 350°F. Grease tart pan with removable bottom, about 9 × 1-inch, or springform pan, 9 × 3-inch. In medium bowl, mix Bisquick mix, powdered sugar and pecans. Cut in butter, using pastry blender (or pulling 2 table knives through mixture in opposite directions), until mixture looks like fine crumbs. Stir in hot water. Press mixture firmly in bottom of tart pan. Bake 15 to 20 minutes or until crust is set but not brown. Brush with ⅓ cup of the preserves. Cool completely.

2 In 1-quart saucepan, heat whipping cream and chocolate chips over medium heat, stirring constantly, until smooth; remove from heat. Stir in liqueur. Pour over crust; spread evenly. Refrigerate at least 2 hours until set.

3 Brush remaining ⅓ cup preserves over chocolate layer. Top with raspberries. Refrigerate at least 15 minutes before serving. Remove side of pan. Cut tart into wedges. Store covered in refrigerator.

High Altitude (3500-6500 ft): Heat oven to 375°F.

1 SERVING: Calories 395 (Calories from Fat 215); Total Fat 24g (Saturated Fat 10g); Cholesterol 20mg; Sodium 250mg; Total: Carbohydrate 46g (Dietary Fiber 4g); Protein 3g

Fudgy Frosted Brownie Cookies

PREP TIME: 1 HOUR 15 MINUTES ▪ **START TO FINISH: 1 HOUR 15 MINUTES**
18 COOKIES

COOKIES

1 cup Original Bisquick mix

³⁄₄ cup granulated sugar

²⁄₃ cup chopped pecans

¹⁄₂ cup unsweetened baking
　　cocoa

¹⁄₂ cup sour cream

1 teaspoon vanilla

1 egg

FROSTING

2 oz unsweetened baking
　　chocolate

2 tablespoons butter or
　　margarine

2 cups powdered sugar

3 to 4 tablespoons hot water

1 Heat oven to 350°F. Spray cookie sheets with cooking spray. In medium bowl, mix all cookie ingredients until well blended.

2 Drop dough by rounded tablespoonfuls about 2 inches apart on cookie sheets.

3 Bake 9 to 11 minutes or until set. Cool 2 minutes; remove from cookie sheets to cooling rack. Cool completely, about 30 minutes.

4 In 2-quart saucepan, melt chocolate and butter over low heat, stirring occasionally. Remove from heat. Stir in powdered sugar and 3 tablespoons of the hot water until smooth. (If frosting is too thick, add additional water, 1 teaspoon at a time.) Spread frosting over cookies.

High Altitude (3500-6500 ft): No change.

1 COOKIE: Calories 200 (Calories from Fat 80); Total Fat 9g (Saturated Fat 3.5g); Cholesterol 20mg; Sodium 100mg; Total Carbohydrate 29g (Dietary Fiber 2g); Protein 2g

Cappuccino Bars

PREP TIME: 15 MINUTES ● **START TO FINISH: 40 MINUTES**
32 BARS

BARS

1½ cups Original Bisquick mix

1 cup packed brown sugar

½ cup raisins

¼ cup chopped nuts

2 tablespoons instant coffee granules or crystals

½ teaspoon ground cinnamon

½ cup water

2 tablespoons shortening

1 egg

CAPPUCCINO GLAZE

1 cup powdered sugar

¼ teaspoon vanilla

1 to 2 tablespoons cold brewed coffee or milk

1 Heat oven to 350°F. Grease bottom and sides of 13 × 9-inch pan with shortening; lightly flour. In medium bowl, stir all bar ingredients until well blended. Spread in pan.

2 Bake 20 to 25 minutes or until toothpick inserted in center comes out clean.

3 In small bowl, mix all glaze ingredients until smooth and thin enough to drizzle. Drizzle glaze over warm bars. For bars, cut into 8 rows by 4 rows. Serve warm or cool.

High Altitude (3500–6500 ft): Heat oven to 375°F. Decrease Bisquick mix to 1¼ cups and brown sugar to ⅔ cup. Add ¼ cup all-purpose flour with the Bisquick mix.

1 BAR: Calories 90 (Calories from Fat 20); Total Fat 2.5g (Saturated Fat 0.5g); Cholesterol 5mg; Sodium 75mg; Total Carbohydrate 16g (Dietary Fiber 0g); Protein 0g

Glazed Lemon Bars

PREP TIME: 30 MINUTES ▪ START TO FINISH: 2 HOURS
24 BARS

BARS

1 cup Bisquick Heart Smart mix

2 tablespoons powdered sugar

2 tablespoons cold butter or margarine

¾ cup granulated sugar

½ cup fat-free cholesterol-free egg product, 4 egg whites or 2 eggs

1 tablespoon Bisquick Heart Smart mix

2 teaspoons grated lemon peel

2 tablespoons lemon juice

LEMON GLAZE

¾ cup powdered sugar

1 tablespoon plus 1½ teaspoons lemon juice

1 Heat oven to 350°F. In small bowl, mix 1 cup Bisquick mix and the powdered sugar. Cut in butter, using pastry blender or pulling 2 table knives through mixture in opposite directions), until mixture looks like fine crumbs. Press mixture in bottom and ½ inch up edges of ungreased 8-inch square pan. Stir glaze ingredients until smooth. Set aside.

2 Bake about 10 minutes or until light brown. Mix remaining ingredients except glaze ingredients; pour over baked layer.

3 Bake about 25 minutes or until set and golden brown. While warm, loosen edges from sides of pan. Spread with glaze. Cool completely, about 1 hour. For bars, cut into 6 rows by 4 rows.

High Altitude (3500-6500 ft): Use 9 × 9 × 2-inch square pan. Press crust in bottom only of pan. Increase bake time in step 2 to about 12 minutes.

1 BAR: Calories 70 (Calories from Fat 10); Total Fat 1g (Saturated Fat 0g); Cholesterol 0mg; Sodium 80mg; Total Carbohydrate 14g (Dietary Fiber 0g); Protein 1g

Frozen Tiramisu Squares

PREP TIME: 20 MINUTES ■ **START TO FINISH: 5 HOURS 30 MINUTES**
15 SERVINGS

1 cup Original Bisquick mix

½ cup sugar

⅓ cup baking cocoa

1 tablespoon instant espresso coffee granules

⅓ cup butter or margarine, melted

2 packages (8 oz each) cream cheese, softened

1 can (14 oz) sweetened condensed milk

¼ cup frozen (thawed) orange juice concentrate

1 teaspoon instant espresso coffee granules

1 tablespoon hot water

¼ cup chocolate-flavored syrup

1½ cups whipping (heavy) cream

Baking cocoa, if desired

1 Heat oven to 350°F. Grease 13 × 9-inch pan. In medium bowl, mix Bisquick mix, sugar, ⅓ cup cocoa, 1 tablespoon coffee and the butter until crumbly. Crumble mixture lightly into pan. Bake 6 minutes; cool.

2 In medium bowl, beat cream cheese with electric mixer on medium speed until smooth. Gradually beat in milk. Place about 2 cups of the cream cheese mixture in separate bowl. Add juice concentrate to cream cheese mixture in one bowl. Dissolve 1 teaspoon coffee in hot water; stir coffee mixture and chocolate syrup into cream cheese mixture in other bowl.

3 In chilled medium bowl, beat whipping cream on high speed until stiff. Fold half of the whipped cream into each cream cheese mixture. Cover and refrigerate chocolate mixture. Spoon orange mixture over crust.

4 Freeze crust with orange mixture about 1 hour or until firm. Spread chocolate mixture evenly over orange mixture. Freeze about 4 hours or until firm. Let stand 10 minutes at room temperature before serving. For squares, cut into 5 rows by 3 rows. Sprinkle each serving with cocoa. Store covered in freezer.

High Altitude (3500–6500 ft): No change.

1 SERVING: Calories 420 (Calories from Fat 245); Total Fat 27g (Saturated Fat 14g); Cholesterol 70mg; Sodium 320mg; Total Carbohydrate 38g (Dietary Fiber 1g); Protein 7g

Banana S'mores

¾ cup graham cracker crumbs

½ cup Original Bisquick mix

2 tablespoons sugar

¼ cup butter or margarine, melted

2 medium bananas

2 tablespoons lemon juice

1⅓ cups milk

1 box (4-serving size) vanilla or chocolate instant pudding and pie filling mix

¾ cup miniature marshmallows

½ cup miniature semisweet chocolate chips

1 In small bowl, mix graham cracker crumbs, Bisquick mix and sugar. Stir in butter until moistened. Press in bottom of ungreased 8-inch square microwavable dish. Microwave uncovered on High 1 minute 30 seconds to 3 minutes, rotating dish ½ turn every minute, until crust bubbles up slightly and then begins to flatten. Cool 10 minutes on cooling rack.

2 Peel and slice bananas; dip into lemon juice. Arrange on cooled crust.

3 Beat milk and dry pudding mix with wire whisk or electric mixer on low speed until smooth. Stir in marshmallows. Spread over bananas. Sprinkle with chocolate chips. Refrigerate up to 1 hour before serving. Refrigerate any remaining s'mores.

High Altitude (3500–6500 ft): No change.

1 SERVING: Calories 350 (Calories from Fat 110); Total Fat 12g (Saturated Fat 9g); Cholesterol 25mg; Sodium 520mg; Total Carbohydrate 59g (Dietary Fiber 2g); Protein 4g

Helpful Nutrition
and Cooking Information

Nutrition Guidelines

We provide nutrition information for each recipe that includes calories, fat, cholesterol, sodium, carbohydrate, fiber and protein. Individual food choices can be based on this information.

Recommended intake for a daily diet of 2,000 calories as set by the Food and Drug Administration

Total Fat	Less than 65g
Saturated Fat	Less than 20g
Cholesterol	Less than 300mg
Sodium	Less than 2,400mg
Total Carbohydrate	300g
Dietary Fiber	25g

CRITERIA USED FOR CALCULATING NUTRITION INFORMATION

- The first ingredient was used wherever a choice is given (such as ⅓ cup sour cream or plain yogurt).

- The first ingredient amount was used wherever a range is given (such as 3- to 3½–pound cut-up broiler-fryer chicken).

- The first serving number was used wherever a range is given (such as 4 to 6 servings).

- "If desired" ingredients and recipe variations were not included (such as sprinkle with brown sugar, if desired).

- Only the amount of a marinade or frying oil that is estimated to be absorbed by the food during preparation or cooking was calculated.

INGREDIENTS USED IN RECIPE TESTING AND NUTRITION CALCULATIONS

- Ingredients used for testing represent those that the majority of consumers use in their homes: large eggs, 2% milk, 80%-lean ground beef, canned ready-to-use chicken broth and vegetable oil spread containing not less than 65 percent fat.

- Fat-free, low-fat or low-sodium products were not used, unless otherwise indicated.

- Solid vegetable shortening (not butter, margarine, nonstick cooking sprays or vegetable oil spread as they can cause sticking problems) was used to grease pans, unless otherwise indicated.

EQUIPMENT USED IN RECIPE TESTING

We use equipment for testing that the majority of consumers use in their homes. If a specific piece of equipment (such as a wire whisk) is necessary for recipe success, it is listed in the recipe.

- Cookware and bakeware without nonstick coatings were used, unless otherwise indicated.

- No dark-colored, black or insulated bakeware was used.

- When a pan is specified in a recipe, a metal pan was used; a baking dish or pie plate means ovenproof glass was used.

- An electric hand mixer was used for mixing only when mixer speeds are specified in the recipe directions. When a mixer speed is not given, a spoon or fork was used.

COOKING TERMS GLOSSARY

Beat: Mix ingredients vigorously with spoon, fork, wire whisk, hand beater or electric mixer until smooth and uniform.

Boil: Heat liquid until bubbles rise continuously and break on the surface and steam is given off. For rolling boil, the bubbles form rapidly.

Chop: Cut into coarse or fine irregular pieces with a knife, food chopper, blender or food processor.

Cube: Cut into squares ½ inch or larger.

Dice: Cut into squares smaller than ½ inch.

Grate: Cut into tiny particles using small rough holes of grater (citrus peel or chocolate).

Grease: Rub the inside surface of a pan with shortening, using pastry brush, piece of waxed paper or paper towel, to prevent food from sticking during baking (as for some casseroles).

Julienne: Cut into thin, matchlike strips, using knife or food processor (vegetables, fruits, meats).

Mix: Combine ingredients in any way that distributes them evenly.

Sauté: Cook foods in hot oil or margarine over medium-high heat with frequent tossing and turning motion.

Shred: Cut into long thin pieces by rubbing food across the holes of a shredder, as for cheese, or by using a knife to slice very thinly, as for cabbage.

Simmer: Cook in liquid just below the boiling point on top of the stove; usually after reducing heat from a boil. Bubbles will rise slowly and break just below the surface.

Stir: Mix ingredients until uniform consistency. Stir once in a while for stirring occasionally, often for stirring frequently and continuously for stirring constantly.

Toss: Tumble ingredients (such as green salad) lightly with a lifting motion, usually to coat evenly or mix with another food.

Metric Conversion Guide

VOLUME

U.S. Units	Canadian Metric	Australian Metric
1/4 teaspoon	1 mL	1 ml
1/2 teaspoon	2 mL	2 ml
1 teaspoon	5 mL	5 ml
1 tablespoon	15 mL	20 ml
1/4 cup	50 mL	60 ml
1/3 cup	75 mL	80 ml
1/2 cup	125 mL	125 ml
2/3 cup	150 mL	170 ml
3/4 cup	175 mL	190 ml
1 cup	250 mL	250 ml
1 quart	1 liter	1 liter
1 1/2 quarts	1.5 liters	1.5 liters
2 quarts	2 liters	2 liters
2 1/2 quarts	2.5 liters	2.5 liters
3 quarts	3 liters	3 liters
4 quarts	4 liters	4 liters

WEIGHT

U.S. Units	Canadian Metric	Australian Metric
1 ounce	30 grams	30 grams
2 ounces	55 grams	60 grams
3 ounces	85 grams	90 grams
4 ounces (1/4 pound)	115 grams	125 grams
8 ounces (1/2 pound)	225 grams	225 grams
16 ounces (1 pound)	455 grams	500 grams
1 pound	455 grams	1/2 kilogram

MEASUREMENTS

Inches	Centimeters
1	2.5
2	5.0
3	7.5
4	10.0
5	12.5
6	15.0
7	17.5
8	20.5
9	23.0
10	25.5
11	28.0
12	30.5
13	33.0

TEMPERATURES

Fahrenheit	Celsius
32°	0°
212°	100°
250°	120°
275°	140°
300°	150°
325°	160°
350°	180°
375°	190°
400°	200°
425°	220°
450°	230°
475°	240°
500°	260°

NOTE: The recipes in this cookbook have not been developed or tested using metric measures. When converting recipes to metric, some variations in quality may be noted.

Index

Page numbers in *italics* indicate illustrations